United Nation Scientific and Cultural (

This book traces the history of UNESCO from its foundational idealism to its current stature as the pre-eminent international organization for science, education, and culture, building a well-rounded understanding of this important organization.

The book:

- provides an overview of the organization and its institutional architecture in the context of its humanistic idealism;
- details the subsequent challenges UNESCO faced through the Cold War and power politics, global dependence and interdependence, and the rise of identity and culture in global politics;
- analyzes the functioning of UNESCO administration, finance, and its various constituencies including the secretariat, member states, and civil society;
- explores the major controversies and issues underlying the initiatives in education, science, culture and communication;
- examines the current agenda and future challenges through three major issues in UNESCO: Education for All, digital divide issues, and norms on cultural diversity;
- assesses the role of UNESCO in making norms in a complex world of multiple actors and intersecting issue areas.

Reflecting on UNESCO's vision, its everyday practices, and future challenges, this work is an essential resource for students and scholars of international relations and international organizations.

J. P. Singh is Associate Professor at the graduate program in Communication, Culture and Technology at Georgetown University, USA.

Routledge Global Institutions

Edited by Thomas G. Weiss
The CUNY Graduate Center, New York, USA
and Rorden Wilkinson
University of Manchester, UK

About the series

The "Global Institutions Series" is designed to provide readers with comprehensive, accessible, and informative guides to the history, structure, and activities of key international organizations as well as books that deal with topics of key importance in contemporary global governance. Every volume stands on its own as a thorough and insightful treatment of a particular topic, but the series as a whole contributes to a coherent and complementary portrait of the phenomenon of global institutions at the dawn of the millennium.

Books are written by recognized experts, conform to a similar structure, and cover a range of themes and debates common to the series. These areas of shared concern include the general purpose and rationale for organizations, developments over time, membership, structure, decision-making procedures, and key functions. Moreover, current debates are placed in historical perspective alongside informed analysis and critique. Each book also contains an annotated bibliography and guide to electronic information as well as any annexes appropriate to the subject matter at hand.

The volumes currently published are:

46 United Nations Educational, Scientific and Cultural Organization (UNESCO) (2010)
Creating Norms for a Complex World
by J. P. Singh (Georgetown University)

45 The International Labour Organization (2010)
Coming In from the Cold
by Steve Hughes (Newcastle University) and Nigel Haworth (University of Auckland)

44 Global Poverty (2010)
How Global Governance Is Failing the Poor
by David Hulme (University of Manchester)

UNICEF
by Richard Jolly (University of Sussex)

The Organization of American States (OAS)
by Mônica Herz (Instituto de Relações Internacionais)v

FIFA
by Alan Tomlinson (University of Brighton)

International Law, International Relations, and Global Governance
by Charlotte Ku (University of Illinois, College of Law)

Humanitarianism Contested
by Michael Barnett (George Washington University) and Thomas G. Weiss (The CUNY Graduate Center)

Forum on China-Africa Cooperation (FOCAC)
by Ian Taylor (University of St. Andrews)

The Bank for International Settlements
The politics of global financial supervision in the age of high finance
by Kevin Ozgercin (SUNY College at Old Westbury)

International Migration
by Khalid Koser (Geneva Centre for Security Policy)

Global Health Governance
by Sophie Harman (City University, London)

Global Think Tanks
Policy networks and governance
by James McGann (University of Pennsylvania) with Richard Sabatini

The Council of Europe
by Martyn Bond (University of London)

The United Nations Development Programme (UNDP)
by Stephen Browne (The International Trade Centre, Geneva)

International Aid
by Paul Mosley (University of Sheffield)

Maritime Piracy
by Bob Haywood

Religious Institutions and Global Politics
by Katherine Marshall (Georgetown University)

South Asian Association for Regional Cooperation (SAARC)
by Lawrence Saez (University of London)

The International Trade Centre
by Stephen Browne (The Future of the UN Development System (FUNDS) Project, Geneva) and Samuel Laird (University of Nottingham)

The Group of Twenty (G20)
by Andrew F. Cooper (Centre for International Governance Innovation, Ontario) and Ramesh Thakur (Balsillie School of International Affairs, Ontario)

The UN Human Rights Council
by Bertrand G. Ramcharan (Geneva Graduate Institute of International and Development Studies)

The International Monetary Fund
Politics of conditional lending, second edition
by James Raymond Vreeland (Georgetown University)

The UN Global Compact
By Catia Gregoratti (Lund University)

Security Governance in Regional Organizations
Edited by Emil Kirchner (University of Essex) and Roberto Dominguez (Suffolk University)

Responsibility to Protect
Perspectives from the Global South
by Thomas G. Weiss (The CUNY Graduate Center) and Rama Mani (University of Oxford)

UN Institutions for Women's Rights
by Charlotte Patton (York College, CUNY) and Carolyn Stephenson (University of Hawaii)

For further information regarding the series, please contact:

Craig Fowlie, Senior Publisher, Politics & International Studies
Taylor & Francis
2 Park Square, Milton Park, Abingdon
Oxon OX14 4RN, UK

+44 (0)207 842 2057 Tel
+44 (0)207 842 2302 Fax

Craig.Fowlie@tandf.co.uk
www.routledge.com

United Nations Educational, Scientific and Cultural Organization (UNESCO)

Creating norms for a complex world

J. P. Singh

Routledge
Taylor & Francis Group

LONDON AND NEW YORK

First published 2011
by Routledge
2 Park Square, Milton Park, Abingdon, Oxon, OX14 4RN

Simultaneously published in the U.S.A. and Canada
by Routledge
270 Madison Avenue, New York, NY 10016

Routledge is an imprint of the Taylor & Francis Group, an informa business

© 2011 J. P. Singh

Typeset in Times New Roman by
Taylor & Francis Books
Printed and bound in Great Britain by
TJ International Ltd, Padstow, Cornwall

British Library Cataloguing in Publication Data
A catalogue record for this book is available from the British Library

Library of Congress Cataloging in Publication Data
Singh, J. P., 1961–
  United Nations Educational, Scientific, and Cultural Organization
(UNESCO): Creating norms for a complex world / J.P. Singh.
    p. cm. – (Routledge global institutions)1. Unesco. I. Title.
  AS4.U83S56 2010
  001.06'01–dc22
                              2010021069

ISBN 978-0-415-49113-6 (hbk)
ISBN 978-0-415-49114-3 (pbk)
ISBN 978-0-203-83858-7 (ebk)

**For Chuck and my mother
for their love and support**

Contents

Illustrations

Tables

Figures

Boxes

Foreword

The current volume is the forty-fourth new title—two have already gone into second editions—in a dynamic series on "global institutions." The series strives (and, based on the volumes published to date, succeeds) to provide readers with definitive guides to the most visible aspects of what many of us know as "global governance." Remarkable as it may seem, there exist relatively few books that offer in-depth treatments of prominent global bodies, processes, and associated issues, much less an entire series of concise and complementary volumes. Those that do exist are either out of date, inaccessible to the non-specialist reader, or seek to develop a specialized understanding of particular aspects of an institution or process rather than offer an overall account of its functioning. Similarly, existing books have often been written in highly technical language or have been crafted "in-house" and are notoriously self-serving and narrow.

The advent of electronic media has undoubtedly helped research and teaching by making data and primary documents of international organizations more widely available, but it has also complicated matters. The growing reliance on the Internet and other electronic methods of finding information about key international organizations and processes has served, ironically, to limit the educational and analytical materials to which most readers have ready access—namely, books. Public relations documents, raw data, and loosely refereed web sites do not make for intelligent analysis. Official publications compete with a vast amount of electronically available information, much of which is suspect because of its ideological or self-promoting slant. Paradoxically, a growing range of purportedly independent web sites offering analyses of the activities of particular organizations has emerged, but one inadvertent consequence has been to frustrate access to basic, authoritative, readable, critical, and well-researched texts. The market for such has actually been reduced by the ready availability of varying quality electronic materials.

For those of us who teach, research, and practice in the area, such limited access to information has been frustrating. We were delighted when Routledge saw the value of a series that bucks this trend and provides key reference points to the most significant global institutions and issues. They are betting that serious students and professionals will want serious analyses. We have assembled a first-rate line-up of authors to address that market. Our intention, then, is to provide one-stop shopping for all readers—students (both undergraduate and postgraduate), negotiators, diplomats, practitioners from nongovernmental and intergovernmental organizations, and interested parties alike—seeking information about the most prominent institutional aspects of global governance.

UNESCO

Many books in our Global Institutions series focus on topics relevant for the pursuit of economic and social development—indeed, virtually all of them. We were particularly keen, however, to deal with some of the "softest" of the issues normally classified under the rubric of "low politics," and so the United Nations Educational, Scientific and Cultural Organization (UNESCO) has been high on our list of essential topics for the series. We are fortunate that J. P. Singh agreed to our challenge to author a volume on this topic.

Out of all of the institutions comprising the UN family, UNESCO is familiar to hundreds of millions of individuals worldwide who have visited World Heritage Sites or benefited from textbooks and histories commissioned over the last 65 years, on the one hand, or been offended by the attempt to establish the New World Information Order—which led to the withdrawal from the organization of the United States, the United Kingdom, and Singapore—or else the wasteful spending habits of former directors-general. At the same time, while most people have only the foggiest idea of what lies behind the name, they are quite unaware of the actual nature of the organization or the ideas and values behind its founding.

"States parties to this Constitution, believing in full and equal opportunities for education for all, in the unrestricted pursuit of objective truth, and in the free exchange of ideas and knowledge," states UNESCO's founding document adopted by the London Conference in November 1945, "are agreed and determined to develop and to increase the means of communication between their peoples and to employ these means for the purposes of mutual understanding and a truer and more perfect knowledge of each other's lives."

Of course, knowledge is certainly the base for human progress, and hence the basis for peace among individuals, communities, and states. Yet, UNESCO's pursuit of education, science, and culture has often been anything except non-controversial. There is little in common between the world of London in 1945 and our own—educational, scientific, and cultural realities have not stood still any more than economic, political, military, and economic ones.

J. P. Singh, an Associate Professor in Communication, Culture and Technology at Georgetown University, in Washington, DC, has jumped into this maelstrom and sought to make sense not only of UNESCO's institutional contributions to contemporary global governance but also the nature of educational, scientific, and cultural challenges of the twenty-first century. This he does with aplomb. J. P. has put together one of the most elegantly written and informative, yet appropriately critical books on UNESCO to date, and we are pleased to have it in the Global Institutions series.

J. P. was an obvious choice for us to approach to write this book. A first-rate scholar with six books (authored and edited)[1] under his belt and a string of publications in leading journals, he has an inside track on UNESCO through his membership of the UNESCO Task Force for Cultural Statistics and his membership of UNESCO's Expert Group on the Measurement of the Diversity of Cultural Expressions. J. P.'s capacity to reflect critically on the tale of such a curious institution is not, however, compromised by this inside track. Quite the contrary, it has enabled him to sharpen his analysis such that the end product offers one of the most compelling and comprehensive accounts of the organization. In crafting this book, J. P. has also clearly underlined why better understanding the softer institutions of global governance is as important as focusing on the more notable and notorious headline grabbers.

We thoroughly recommend this book to all interested in the study of world politics, international organization, global governance, and cultural governance, diversity and change. As always, we look forward to comments from first-time or veteran readers of the Global Institutions series.

Thomas G. Weiss, The CUNY Graduate Center, New York, USA
Rorden Wilkinson, University of Manchester, UK
May 2010

Acknowledgements

Most of us are introduced to UNESCO while visiting the World Heritage Sites, now 890 of them in 148 countries. We find, usually at the entrance of the site, a sign that announces the site's universal and outstanding value. I was elated to learn in 2008, while writing this book, that the 96-kilometer Kalka-Shimla railway line in North India, on which I have traveled since childhood, is now inscripted on the World Heritage list as part of Mountain Railways of India. The British empire's administrators built this railway line as part of connecting the enterprise of the Raj with India House in London, especially as they took to moving the capital of the Raj to Simla (the old spelling) every summer starting in 1864. The railway line was built in the mid-nineteenth century. Simla also had a telegraph link with London by 1870.

I suspect that depending on whether you are a government official, a diplomat, a civil society organization staffer, a scientist, an educator, or a communications specialist, you have been exposed to one or more features of UNESCO while growing up. It retains a prominent stature among UN specialized agencies and, as the following pages show, draws it strengths from the power of its intellectual debates and its moral and ethical position in the world.

Over the years, my other contacts with UNESCO, albeit from an intellectual distance, included studying the feisty debates on the New World Information Communication Order (NWICO) in the 1980s that questioned the communication order or, in the words of its supporters, the neo-colonial communication empire that replaced the old one. My interest in development exposed me to the report from the World Commission on Culture and Development, which UN secretary-general Javier Pérez de Cuéllar headed. A few years later, the report's lessons were applied to another passionate debate at UNESCO, this time on culture and trade. This issue pitted the United States and Hollywood against a coalition of cultural industries and policy-makers from around the world led by France and Canada. Writing about this last debate, and participating in two groups at the UNESCO Institute for Statistics on cultural statistics, introduced me to officials at UNESCO offices in Paris and in Montreal who were far more willing to indulge in interdisciplinary and intellectual debates than the organization to which I had paid most scholarly attention until then, namely the World Trade Organization (WTO). At the WTO, someone told me once, everything has a dollar value and all prerogatives can be translated to tariffs and trade protections. At UNESCO, such instrumental monetary calculations are derided, although the organization has a hard time defining its identity beyond its compelling preamble statement regarding constructing the defenses of peace in the minds of human beings.

I am indebted to Rorden Wilkinson for encouraging me to write this book and to Tom Weiss for providing various kinds of assistance and good cheer along the way. Thanks to Nicola Parkin for her patient reminders and help. Thanks to Martin Burke and Megan Graieg for seeing me to the finish line. As I headed into the final phase of writing, I worried that I needed to corroborate my analysis with more materials from first hand exposure to UNESCO offices. UNESCO officials told me that I would be best placed to make my contacts via the US Mission to UNESCO because they prefer academics to be recommended by their home governments! It was as if a god of research and scholarship—perhaps Pallas Athena of UNESCO's emblem—heard me. A week later I received an invitation from the US State Department for the swearing-in of the Obama administration's ambassador-designate to UNESCO, David Killion. I wondered if this was the same David Killion with whom I taught international relations in 1992–93 at Scripps College, Claremont. Both graduate students at that time, we were, in fact, the Department of International Relations—David Killion taught security and theory and I taught international political economy, development, and international ethnic politics. Our paths had converged again, this time in the "real world" of international relations, namely UNESCO.

I cannot thank enough Ambassador Killion, the US Department of State, and various officials at UNESCO for making available numerous resources and sharing their ideas in frank and open conversations. If I am in any way critical in the following pages, of the UNESCO secretariat or of US engagements with UNESCO, it is because I am a scholar and my task is to analyze and provide a perspective for understanding these engagements. Fortunately, there's also much to praise both within UNESCO and in other countries' engagement with it. The United States left UNESCO in 1983 amidst NWICO and other politicized controversies, and rejoined in 2003. At his swearing-in, Ambassador

Killion said that "the United States remains committed to working through the Organization to advance education for all, support science and engineering, preserve the world's heritage, and promote freedom of expression, gender equality, human rights, and tolerance." As UNESCO confronts a new century and new politics, it has a great deal to offer in these and other complex issues.

My thanks also to Ambassador Killion's staff, especially Holly Hubler, for its generous assistance. Director-General (DG) Kōichiro Matsuura and his office provided all manner of help. DG Matsuura noted at our meeting that he looked forward to a book on UNESCO from an American perspective. While my perspective regarding UNESCO has been shaped as much by the Kalka-Shimla railway line connecting my hometown to an old empire as it is by teaching a bicycle ride away from the White House, I hope that I have, at least, tried to provide a "balanced" perspective in the following pages, even if it is chiefly "American" and definitely not from someone who is a UNESCO "insider." At UNESCO, I express my gratitude to Giuomar Alonso Cano, Anne Candau, Cécile Duvelle, Jonathan Baker, Nicholas Burnett, Ricardo de Guimarães Pinto, Walter Erdelen, Kang "Rock" S. Huang, Elizabeth Longworth, Françoise Rivière, Pierre Sané, Mogens Schmidt, and Susan Schneegans. I have gained immensely from participating in UNESCO Institute of Statistics' (UIS) Cultural Statistics Taskforce and the Expert Group on Measuring the Diversity of Cultural Expressions. At UIS, I thank Simon Ellis, José Pessoa, and Lydia Deloumeaux. At the US Department of State, my thanks to Elizabeth Kanick, Kelly Seikman, and Laura Gritz. I have also gained from my conversations with various scholars interested in UNESCO issues and would in particular like to thank Françoise Benhamou, Tyler Cowen, Phyllis Magrab, and Vijayendra Rao.

Georgetown's interdisciplinary program on Communication, Culture and Technology parallels the interdisciplinary approaches in UNESCO and has thus been a perfect home from where to contemplate this book. Three tireless, smart, and (very) enthusiastic research assistants at Georgetown University furnished materials, read drafts, and collected data for me. For all this and more, a big word of thanks to Anuj Gurung, Hillá Meller, and Becky Jakob. My thanks to the Conflict Resolution Program at Georgetown, especially Fathali Moghaddam and Craig Zelizer, for making available research resources. My colleague Katherine Marshall's advice from having written the book on the World Bank in this series was enormously helpful.

Finally, as always, my partner Chuck Johnson's continued guidance and support for everything I do means the world to me. Daily telephone calls to my mother also produced "external accountability" as she kept up with the progress of this book. In appreciation, I finished writing this book on her birthday, and completed the revisions on the day that she had been watching a TV program in India on UNESCO World Book and Copyright Day and proceeded to wish me, "happy copyright day." UNESCO has a way of reaching people all around the world! Lastly, I thank many friends who continue to believe, even when I don't, that this world can be a better place and they remain an inspiration.

This book has allowed me to bring together and connect my old and new experiences with UNESCO as the organization works toward a culture of peace. I hope that it does the same for you.

Abbreviations

ADG	Assistant director-general
AMARC	World Association of Community Broadcasters
APC	Association for Progressive Communication
ASNE	American Society of Newspaper Editors
ASPNet	Associated Schools Project
BIE	Bureau of International Education
CAME	Conference of Allied Ministers in Education
C&I	Communication and information sector
COMEST	World Commission on the Ethics of Scientific Knowledge and Technology
CRIS	Communication Rights for an Information Society
DAC	Development Assistance Committee (OECD)
DBS	Direct broadcasting satellites
DG	Director-General
ECOSOC	Economic and Social Council (UN)
EFA	Education for All initiative
FAO	Food and Agriculture Organization
GATT	General Agreement on Tariffs and Trade
GEF	Global Environmental Fund
GLOSS	Global Sea Level Observing System
GOOS	Global Ocean Observing System
IACOMS	International Advisory Committee on Marine Science
IAEA	International Atomic Energy Agency
IAHS	International Association of Hydrological Sciences
IBC	International Bioethics Committee
IBSP	International Basic Science Program
ICANN	Internet Corporation for Assigned Names and Numbers
ICESCR	International Covenant on Economic, Social and Cultural Rights

ICSU	International Council of Science (formerly International Council of Scientific Unions; current title maintains the old acronym)
ICT	Information and communication technology
IGBC	Intergovernmental Bioethics Committee
IGOSS	Integrated Global Ocean Stations System
IGSP	International Geosciences Program
IHP	International Hydrological Programme
IIEP	International Institute for Educational Planning
IIIC	International Institute for Intellectual Cooperation
IMO	International Maritime Organization
INCD	International Network for Cultural Diversity
INCP	International Network for Cultural Policy
INGO	International non-governmental organization
IOC	Intergovernmental Oceanographic Commission
IOTWS	Indian Ocean Tsunami Early Warning System
IPDC	International Program for the Development of Communication
ISP	International Science Programmes
ITU	International Telecommunications Union
IUCN	World Conservation Union
IUGS	International Union of Geological Scientists
MAB	Man and the Biosphere program
MOST	Management of Social Transformations program
NAM	Non-Aligned Movement
NGO	Non-governmental organization
NIEO	New International Economic Order
NWICO	New World Information and Communication Order
OECD	Organization for Economic Co-operation and Development
PTWS	Pacific Tsunami Warning System
RBM	Results-based management
SCFIP	Sub-Commission on Freedom of Information and of the Press
SESAME	Synchrotron-light for Experimental Science and Applications in the Middle East
SHS	Social and human sciences
UDHR	Universal Declaration of Human Rights
UIS	Institute for Statistics (UNESCO)
UNCLOS	UN Conference on the Law of the Sea
UNCTAD	United Nations Conference on Trade and Development
UNDP	United Nations Development Programme

UNEP	United Nations Environmental Programme
UNESCO	United Nations Educational, Scientific and Cultural Organization
UNICEF	United Nations Children's Fund
UNIDO	United Nations Industrial Development Organization
UNRWA	United Nations Relief Works Agency
USSR	Union of Soviet Socialist Republics
WARC	World Administrative Radio Conference
WGIG	Working Group on Internet Governance
WHC	World Heritage Centre
WHO	World Health Organization
WIPO	World Intellectual Property Organization
WMO	World Meteorological Association
WSIS	World Summit on the Information Society

Introduction

> That since wars begin in the minds of men, it is in the minds of men that the defences of peace must be constructed.
>
> Preamble to the UNESCO Constitution

The United Nations Educational, Scientific and Cultural Organization represents both the hopes and the limits of human endeavors at creating norms for a peaceful world. At its best, UNESCO is the heroic intellectual and moral force of the idealism encapsulated in its Preamble. This idealism seeks to educate humanity to overcome its worst self through cultural dialogues, scientific collaborations, literacy, and communication. At its worst, UNESCO, like many other UN agencies, is a functional tragedy of our own making, suffering from power politics, lack of resources, ineffectiveness, and managerial ineptitude.

UNESCO came into being after a conference of delegates from 37 countries met on 1–16 November 1945, in London, and 20 signed on to the constitution. This conference framed a charter reflecting three years of diplomacy, begun among the Allied Powers, to institute a post-war organization that would reflect enlightenment values in seeking to end human violence through education. As the negotiations proceeded beyond 1942, the emphasis on education was expanded to include science and culture as central tenets of the emerging institution. Speaking to the London Conference, the British Prime Minister Clement Attlee, asked the important question, "Do not all wars begin in the minds of men?" The US delegate to the conference Archibald Macleish, Librarian of Congress, adapted these words for the Preamble of the UNESCO Constitution (see the Appendix for UNESCO Preamble and Constitution).

UNESCO continues to embody a humanism borne of the Enlightenment in a twenty-first century intellectual milieu uneasy with grand narratives, especially when they arise from the minds of the privileged and the few. At its core, UNESCO reflects a scientific humanism "in the sense that the application of science provides most of the material basis for human culture, and also that the practice and the understanding of science needs to be integrated with that of other human activities," to quote Julian Huxley, its first director-general.[1] To its credit, UNESCO has dodged the controversies about its master narratives through its convening power of bringing together the world's intellectuals of all ideological hues, even if at times one particular ideology may be dominant in its ranks. From Albert Einstein to Wole Soyinka, intellectual luminaries have lent their weight to an organization with an encompassing agenda but a limited mandate in terms of its resources. This chapter describes three central tensions underlying UNESCO's norm-making capacity. These tensions also inform the main argument of the book, which balances UNESCO's high philosophy with its more mundane functional aspects through its history.

Idealism and power

UNESCO's philosophical leaning comes through in its norm creation role, which can be understood "as a standard of appropriate behavior for actors with a given identity."[2] Norm formation standards generally carry a sense of the just, the good, and the ethical. UNESCO is explicit in its mission to shape ethical and just norms. Herein perhaps lies the first tension. Actors might agree to the broad philosophical principles that guide the shape of the norm but subsequently disagree on the exact ways to implement it. Different cultural understandings among groups may also lead to contested norms.[3] Given various cultural understandings, the broad consensus toward humanism in UNESCO's Constitution may be traced to two factors: the intellectual history of humanism and the overbearing shadow of the two great wars. Both of these factors, as explained in this sub-section and later, were tempered by rivalries among states and other actors.

The philosophical antecedents of UNESCO can be located in just about every prominent humanist thinker of modern European history. At the broadest level, the idea that human virtue is acquired rather than inherited or that society and governance are better off with the practice of virtue, can be traced back to Beldassare Castiliogne's *Book of the Courtiers* (1528) and Niccolo Machiavelli's *The Prince* (1532). Over the next 400 years, the idea of virtue would spread through the proliferation of education, which advanced from being the privilege of the few to being considered a necessity or even a right for all by the

twentieth century. Humanist pedagogies informed a scientific understanding of human nature, which assigned considerable agency to an
individual's station in life through the acquisition of wisdom. Three
prominent thinkers are often cited as providing the foundation for
UNESCO's humanism: Emmanuel Kant, Auguste Comte, and Jan
Amos Comenius.

Kant's treatise *Perpetual Peace* (1775) envisioned enlightened and
free republics forming a league or a federation of states, which could
eventually abolish standing armies and move toward world citizenship.
Kant's *Perpetual Peace* reflected directly and indirectly the burgeoning
role of diplomacy in the foreign affairs of states. François de Callières
had envisioned a prominent role for diplomacy in which he posited
European states "as being joined together by all kinds of necessary
commerce, in such a way that they may be regarded as members of one
Republic."[4] While Kant wrote of republics, Rousseau wrote of the general
will governing the affairs of the states, which would in turn move these
free states toward democratic peace. By the time of Woodrow Wilson's
Fourteen Points speech to the US Congress on 8 January 1918, the
notion of democracy was firmly entrenched in many Western states.
Wilson's "open covenants of peace, openly arrived at" through diplomacy affirmed this worldview, which emerged at a time when states
began to think of an international organization that would lead by a
rationale rooted in education.

UNESCO's philosophy is also located in deeper spiritual precepts
connected to a human quest for a better world. Vincenzo Pavone provides a compelling account of the almost puritanical ideas of the Czech-
born Comenius (1592–1670) who wrote *The Labyrinth of the World
and the Paradise of the Heart* (1623): "Through education, the Labyrinth
of the World could eventually be reconciled with the Paradise of the
Heart."[5] The puritanical dualism being evoked here is that of a human's
base, violent versus the religious virtuous self. Scientific education was
considered necessary in Comenius' and later Puritanical ideas as leading to the highest state of knowledge and a universal community.
Comenius' influence began to be explicitly acknowledged as antecedent
to UNESCO during Federico Mayor's director-generalship (1987–99),
and was most visible in Mayor's Culture of Peace program, which began
in 1989. UNESCO had published Comenius' collected works in 1956,
and his biography was published in 1991 shortly before the 400th anniversary of his birth. Director-General Mayor frequently cited Comenius
in his speeches, noting at the time of the publication of his biography:
"As Comenius reminds us, the teachers are the key of the future and
the shaper of democracy."[6] Mayor recalled Comenius' notion of

Dicasterium Pacis or world assembly for nations and a *Collegium Lacis*, which would house scholarly members, to name Comenius "as one of the spiritual ancestors of UNESCO."[7]

Similarly to Comenius' thought, Auguste Comte's (1798–1857) "Religion of Humanity" ascribed to science the basis of society and global solidarity that would replace God as its ordering principle. Comte's positivist theory of humanity reflected science to be not just a source for Enlightenment ideas of progress, but also to be its spiritual core. Comte provides a precursor to the ideas of scientific humanism that became popular in the 1930s. Julian Huxley, UNESCO's first director-general (1946–48), tried to provide a similar manifesto in his pamphlet *UNESCO: Its Purpose and Its Philosophy*: "Thus the general philosophy of UNESCO should, it seems, be a scientific world humanism, global in extent and evolutionary in background."[8] The thrust of Huxley's ideas was toward human perfection rooted in natural selection, evolution, and one dangerously close to eugenics. Nevertheless, his ideas also reflected the scientific humanism of the 1930s. In 1933, a group of 33 humanists including academics, philosophers, and theologians, penned a 15-point *Humanist Manifesto*. Point Four noted: "Humanism recognizes that man's religious culture and civilization, as clearly depicted by anthropology and history, are the product of a gradual development due to his interaction with his natural environment and with his social heritage. The individual born into a particular culture is largely molded by that culture."[9]

This humanist thinking and the alternatives it offered sat starkly against the devastation wrought by the two great wars and the effects of Nazism. While most of the post-war thinking shunned ideas of culture, and associated them with the rise of Nazi Germany, UNESCO's architects sought in humanism the seeds of a better culture. "Against the background of this ruined landscape and of the need to rebuild in such a way that this horror would not be repeated, the dominant feeling of UNESCO's founders is readily understandable: they felt a duty to address, as a matter of urgency, the task of reconstituting culture in its material and oral aspects alike."[10] Even as the war progressed, a Conference of Allied Ministers in Education (CAME) met for the first time in 1942 to think of a future international organization in which education would play a key role. CAME ministerials continued until the London Conference in 1945. US Senator Fulbright noted in 1944 at one meeting that education would "do more in the long run for peace than any number of trade treaties."[11]

As the next chapter will show, while the master narrative of humanism and the shadow of the war informed the thinking of CAME and UNESCO's architects, state rivalries also deeply affected the shaping of their statutes. First, there were divisions among the allied ministers themselves and jockeying for influence. Switzerland argued that since the Bureau of International Education (BIE) was located in Geneva, the future international organization to come out of their proceedings should also be located there. France argued for Paris and pointed to the International Institute of Intellectual Cooperation (IIIC). The final bargain locating UNESCO in Paris received British and American endorsement in return for the first director-general, Julian Huxley, being British. Second, the Soviets were skeptical of CAME negotiations and US and British intentions. They were especially opposed to communication becoming any part of the organization's agenda and viewed it as propaganda. It is ironic, that among other issues, the United States would leave UNESCO in 1984 partly due to Soviet control of the communication agenda at UNESCO. Third, philosophically, many opposed the scientific humanist agenda as put forward by Julian Huxley.

While power issues seem relatively minor compared to the high idealism of the humanist philosophy, the former reveal the kinds of forces that would guide UNESCO's everyday business. Nevertheless, the moral force of UNESCO's philosophy and its connection with humanism's past remain the organization's strengths. This past is frequently evoked, for example in Federico Mayor's speeches on Comenius or Julian Huxley's references to ideas of virtue and scientific humanism. The UNESCO emblem, adopted in 1954, evokes this past by abstracting from the temple of Pallas Athena, the goddess of wisdom and reason, atop the Acropolis (Figure I.1). No other post-war organization can command such magnificent evocations of history as UNESCO.

Agenda and pragmatics

Beginning in 1942 the CAME meetings placed significant emphasis on education. The British delegates who convened these conferences envisioned an International Organization for Education. However, all delegates accepted early on that cultural issues would play a role in the organization's future. This was as much due to the denunciation of ideas of racial and cultural purity that existed in Nazi Germany as in the need felt for creating a new culture of peace. If the organization were limited to education and culture, it would have been called UNECO as it was named in the early stages. In fact, officials in the science directorates of UNESCO continue to complain that science has never really been prioritized in the workings of the organization.

Figure I.1 The UNESCO emblem

However, the ways science and communication made it into UNECO are interesting.

CAME established a Science Commission in 1943. Soon, its ideas were linked to the need for a new culture and also a counterweight to German scientific and industrial strength. A Science Commission document noted in 1944: "It is essential that in the new Europe Allied Scientific Culture and outlook shall replace the German."[12] Joseph Needham, a Cambridge biochemist, was particularly important in rallying for the cause of science within the evolving organization and in providing a scientific rationale and methodology for the work of peace. Another important early factor would be the choice of Darwinian biologist Julian Huxley, who would further bridge the gap between science and culture through a doctrine of scientific humanism.

The "C" in UNESCO stands for culture. However, communication and media comprise the fifth sector of the organization after education, natural sciences, human sciences, and culture. From the beginnings of the organization the Soviets opposed the agenda for press and media freedoms backed by Western allied countries, led by the United States. This opposition may account for the USSR not becoming a member of UNESCO until 1954 and for Poland and Czechoslovakia withdrawing their membership in 1947. Nevertheless, a Sub-Commission on Freedom of Information and of the Press (SCFIP) was constituted in 1946, and in 1949 the Economic and Social Council (ECOSOC) of the UN gave it a wide mandate to consider such freedoms from the perspective of human rights.[13] However, SCFIP was dissolved in 1952 and the USSR joined in 1954. In the 1970s and early 1980s, the pendulum of communication and media swung the other way, this time leaning to the left with developing countries and the Soviet bloc accusing the Western world of media hegemony. The United Kingdom and the United States then left UNESCO in 1984–85.

There is no doubt that UNESCO inherited a broad agenda to create a culture of peace through science, education, cultural programs, and communication. Although this agenda may be traced back to Enlightenment philosophical traditions and the great wars, the challenge lies in implementing it through an organization that seems to be divided into five distinct secretariats and competencies. It is one thing to be a moral force in world politics, it is quite another to translate such morality into practice. At a practical level, UNESCO finds itself in intraorganizational battles deciding its priorities and allocating its limited resources. Beyond resource allocation, it is often unclear how the broad mandate of the organization can be translated to the practical level of implementation. What exactly does it mean to create a new culture of peace, for example? Does it require norm formation or also implementation of specific projects? Similarly, the organization must pull its various agencies together for programs that transcend a specific sector. This task creates further practical difficulties.

Multiple actors

While UNESCO includes nearly 200 member-states and observers, it prides itself in also being a philosophical think-tank that can convene the world's intellectuals and civil society to deliberate humanity's most pressing concerns. During the CAME discussions, the French pushed for the creation of a non-governmental organization, and promoted the model of the International Institute of Intellectual Cooperation (IIIC). The French vision would only include the world's intellectuals, but this initiative encountered opposition from the United States and the United Kingdom. UNESCO is now a member-state driven organization but includes intellectuals, civil society, and is intimately linked with other international organizations. These multiple actors speak to both the organization's strengths and weaknesses. Nevertheless, the task of arbitrating multiple pressures is not unique to UNESCO—it is a challenge for global governance in general.

UNESCO scholars agree that the organization resulted from two negotiation processes, one in London and the other in San Francisco, which founded the United Nations. The result was that agencies such as UNESCO would become specialized agencies of the UN's Economic and Social Council (ECOSOC). Articles 63 and 67 of the UN Charter brought these agencies into the UN system. The early directors-general of UNESCO were also avid supporters of the UN system. However, the specialized agencies won support for functional independence of their budgets in terms of getting dues from member states rather than allocations from the UN system. UNESCO would also be subordinate to ECOSOC and subject to UN General Assembly resolutions.

In actuality, UNESCO's role within the UN system is increasingly complicated. As we will see in subsequent chapters, functions that UNESCO performs are overlapped and paralleled in other UN organizations and specialized agencies. Furthermore, it is not a funding or a development organization such as the World Bank. UNESCO must then balance its mandate with the limited role that it can play in actual implementation of its programs. A case in point is the eight Millennium Development Goals framed in 2000 by the 192 members of the UN, one of which is universal primary education and another being gender equity. UNESCO was entrusted as the lead UN agency for fulfilling the education mandate in these two goals but it may not have the resources and staff at the country level to be able to implement the education program. Similarly, UNESCO's recent attempts to link its internal agendas, as in its November 2009 World Report *Investing in Cultural Diversity and Intercultural Dialogue*, to the Millennium Development Goals may be limited by its lack of clout.[14]

The French proposal for a non-governmental organization at the CAME negotiations intersected the desire of the negotiators to involve civil society and intellectuals in constructing peace in the minds of human beings. There were two end results; first, member states agreed to form National Commissions for UNESCO. The United States, for example, constitutes a 100-person National Commission that brings together individuals from federal and state government agencies, non-governmental organizations, and at-large individual members representing civil society. Article 1 of the Charter of the US National Commission for UNESCO states: "The purpose of the US National Commission for UNESCO (the Commission) shall be to serve the Department of State in an advisory capacity with respect to the consideration of issues related to education, science, communications culture, and the formulation and implementation of US policy towards UNESCO."[15] However, organizationally this is problematic for member states. The Commission is located in different ministries in different countries, creating a cultural problem at the level of UNESCO for individuals coming from various ministries. Even if they all agreed to house it in the same ministry, the Commissions by their very nature demand inter-agency coordination, which is not easy for governments to undertake.

Furthermore, for a few countries, it is hard to distinguish between National Commissions and official delegations to UNESCO.

Second, as with ECOSOC, UNESCO would work closely with transnational civil society organizations and intellectuals. As noted before, IIIC was itself a non-governmental organization. So was the International Council of Scientific Unions founded in 1931, of which Joseph Needham was a member, and which boosted the rank of science in UNESCO's functioning. UNESCO would later avow not to duplicate the work of non-governmental organizations to which it lent support such as the International Council of Museums (ICOM) founded by UNESCO in 1946 or the World Worldlife Fund founded in 1961.[16] Beyond its links with non-governmental organizations, UNESCO has forged links with civil society through its ability to convene the world's intellectuals, artists, and celebrities to deliberate human problems or to be its goodwill ambassadors in other places.

Conclusion

Global governance is a difficult task in that it must attend not only to formal rules and charters but also to intersubjective conceptions among various actors.[17] UNESCO's humane philosophy pervades the organization but it is challenging for the organization to control such a wide agenda, which includes managing the intersubjective conceptions among the world's populations as well as the micro-level implementation rules. UNESCO is a long way from realizing the lofty ambitions of its Preamble, which involve implementing initiatives such as universal education, deliberating climate control, propagating press freedoms, inscribing the world's cultural heritage, or shaping ethical guidelines for textbooks on history.

The chapters that follow describe in detail the negotiations that led to UNESCO and its record in its five core sectors: education, natural sciences, social and human sciences, culture, and communication and information. Chapter 1 details UNESCO's organizational mechanics and agendas. It provides the historical context for understanding UNESCO's creation and its subsequent politics before analyzing the functioning of its administration, finance, and its various constituencies including the secretariat, member states, and civil society. The subsequent chapters detail key aspects and controversies underlying the initiatives in education (Chapter 2), sciences (Chapter 3), culture (Chapter 4) and communication (Chapter 5). These chapters provide a broad outline of the activities in each sector. Furthermore Chapters 3–5 discuss at length the particular issues that provided prominence to the sectors. These include: Education for All (EFA, Chapter 2) that rose in the 1990s to finally give life to the universal education ideal to which UNESCO has always aspired, science policies (Chapter 3) in national governments that reflected norms elevating the cause of science at the international level; prominent measures of preserving cultures and heritage through the World Heritage Convention, the Convention for the Protection of Intangible Cultural Heritage, and the Convention for the Protection and Promotion of a Diversity of Cultural Expressions (Chapter 4); and, finally, the New World Information Communication Order (Chapter 5) that led to a North–South conflict over media concentration and information flows that contributed to the withdrawal of the United States, United Kingdom, and Singapore in the 1980s from UNESCO. While in education, culture, and communication, one or two major debates provide a "storyline" for the narrative, the case of the sciences is different: here a patchwork of initiatives and programs rather than a resounding debate or two have guided the sectoral missions.

Sectoral classification is used in Chapters 2–5, but the classification as used in this book is issue-based and practical, and not always specific to organizational divisions within UNESCO. Thus, although UNESCO divides natural and social sciences into separate programs or sectors, here they are presented in one chapter. Many of the initiatives mentioned in Chapters 2–5 within UNESCO may also encompass more than one sector in UNESCO itself. For example, the natural heritage program in UNESCO is administered with help from the natural sciences sector but Chapter 4 in this volume describes it as part of cultural efforts at UNESCO.

The three tensions outlined in this chapter—idealism and power, agenda and pragmatics, and multiple actors—pervade the analysis in all chapters of this book. They are woven through an understanding of UNESCO's role in creating norms in a complex world. I return to the issue of norm formation and complexity in the concluding chapter of the book by offering reflections on UNESCO's vision, its everyday practices, and future challenges.

1 UNESCO's organizational history and structure

> All men of goodwill who have the heavy task of seeking, instructing and informing, have their attention focused on our work. Entire peoples passionately follow our discussions. We must not deceive this great hope of a world profoundly desirous of peace, the problems of which can be resolved only by passing from a material approach to an international and human approach. Let us unite in our efforts to give people reasons to believe in a future more closely conforming to their aspirations and conforming also to the ideal of our Charter.
>
> Jacques Maritain, Chief of the French Delegation Inaugural Meeting of Second UNESCO General Conference Palacio de Bellas Artes. Mexico City, November 6, 1947.[1]

UNESCO inherited the hopeful legacy of humanistic philosophy but also the tragic burden of two great wars. In the last 65 years it has struggled to define its overwhelming sense of purpose through the practical difficulties of running a secretariat, conferring with national delegations and commissions, involving non-state actors, and providing a home to the world's intellectuals. The considerable moral force of UNESCO's ideals has thus been tempered by the politics and functional difficulties of convening global actors to deliberate peace, forge global ethics, and provide a normative agenda for education, science, culture, and communication. Sixty-five years after its establishment, UNESCO has survived the political upheavals of the Cold War, the entry of postcolonial states, the exit of the United Kingdom and United States in 1984–85 and their subsequent re-entry in 1997 and 2003 respectively, and the post-Cold War world of multiple actors and identities.

The first two sections of this chapter provide a brief historical survey of UNESCO's creation and the subsequent political context for the organization's functioning. Next the chapter describes the broad tenets of the five sectors in UNESCO and the international agreements that they have furthered. These sectors are: education, natural sciences, social and human sciences, culture, communication and information. Lastly the chapter takes up the nuts and bolts of UNESCO's bureaucracy and leadership and the way that it works through various conferences, meetings and budgetary processes.

Origins and formation

Thirty-seven governments sent delegations to London from 1–16 November 1945 for the conference that would lead to the foundation of UNESCO. It came into being on 4 November 1946 after the requisite 20 states had signed its Constitution and convened its first General Conference that same year from 19 November to 10 December. The Conference of the Allied Ministers of Education (CAME), whose negotiations led to the foundation of UNESCO, dealt with issues such as the governmental versus non-governmental status of the organization, the place of science on its agenda, and the organization's relationship to the UN system. Archibald MacLeish—poet and Librarian of Congress—headed the US delegation, while the French sent Léon Blum, and Ellen Wilkinson, the UK's Minister of Education, headed her country's delegation.

Richard Butler, president of the British Board of Education, convened the first of the CAME conferences in London on 16 November 1942 to start thinking about coordinating Allied efforts in education after the war and to counter the Axis powers' propaganda while the war proceeded. CAME itself arose from deliberations at the London International Assembly, which allowed for individuals from Allied countries to solve common problems. CAME conference attendees included delegates from Belgium, Czechoslovakia, France, Greece, the Netherlands, Norway, Poland, and Yugoslavia. Other countries, including Australia, Canada, China, India, Luxembourg, New Zealand, South Africa, the USSR and the United States, joined the conference at later dates. The United States joined in 1944. The USSR was not present at the last two conferences as East–West fissures began to develop. Butler originally did not foresee a role for CAME after the war but the private delegates at the London International Assembly issued a resolution for a "United Nations Bureau for Educational Reconstruction" before the second CAME meeting on 18 January 1943.

By 1944, proposals for a post-war organization had come forward. The Geneva-based Bureau of International Education provided a viable model for a member states-driven organization. However, the French championed the model based on the International Institute for

Intellectual Cooperation (IIIC), created in 1925 by the League of Nations and based in Paris.[2] Importantly, the IIIC model offered two bureaucratic innovations that the French favored: the involvement of international non-governmental organizations and the idea that states would be represented from the grassroots, including civil society, through the appointment of National Commissions. The international secretariat, headed by an inter-governmental executive board, would take its direction from National Commissions. The inter-governmental organization solution reflected two political realities. First, the French could not prevail over the British and the United States for a non-governmental organization. Second, delegates considered non-governmental organizations to be weak and felt that member states would not support them with contributions. French intellectual Roger Caillois noted in 1975 that although IIIC attracted such noted figures as Albert Einstein and Sigmund Freud, it was not an effective agency: "They held impressive dialogues with one another, a very elevated correspondence, but neither activity had much hold on the reality of affairs."[3] Contrary to what the French wanted, member states would lead the organization, but French pressures did pay off in other respects: the new organization would be located in Paris, not Geneva, and did have a tripartite structure including INGOs and other civil society bodies. INGOs were to be given formal recognition within UNESCO in order to establish "effective working relationships with such organizations and agencies" (Article XI:I of the UNESCO Constitution). The first INGO to get this recognition was the International Council of Scientific Unions, created in Brussels in 1931 (now known as the International Council of Science although it maintains the acronym ICSU), which had worked closely with IIIC. Furthermore Article VII of the Constitution asked states to set up "National Commissions and National Cooperating Bodies." Brazil was the first country to set up a National Commission in 1946. UNESCO's attempts to accommodate a multi-actor, multi-polar world were incredibly prescient in anticipating the debates raging in global governance during our own time.

Until 1944, the idea of an international organization had centered on a United Nations Educational and Cultural Organization (UNECO). As IIIC had included thinking about cultural exchanges and information, the place of culture was not in doubt. Furthermore, the war itself had highlighted the importance of preserving cultural objects. However, the place of science often got subsumed in other sectors. Initially the interest in "science" was seen as part of the education agenda in a new organization, such as through textbooks and dissemination of scientific knowledge. IIIC had also included a section named Scientific

Information and Scientific Relations. "One recalls the arguments: the pedagogues regarded science as something which, read in text books or taught in class, belonged to education and the aesthetes regarded science as something which, with the grace and patina of time, might qualify as culture."[4]

Scientific communities worked through the CAME processes, initially in calls to balance the German scientific power and, subsequently, in the role of science for reconstruction. CAME established a Commission on Scientific and Laboratory Equipment in October 1943. Known as the Science Commission, it noted in 1944: "It is essential that in the new Europe Allied Scientific Culture and outlook shall replace the German."[5]

Joseph Needham, a Cambridge biochemist, avidly pursued the cause of international scientific cooperation that eventually resulted in the S of UNESCO. In February 1943, Needham, a socialist himself, was sent to China by the Royal Society to strengthen scientific exchanges. In 1944, Needham contacted scientific colleagues around the world and proposed an International Science Cooperation Service. It was during a February 1945 visit to Washington, DC, that Needham convinced the Americans that science deserved a prominent role in what then was known as UNECO. Nevertheless, it was only in the final draft texts at the November 1945 meetings that the world "Scientific" was added to the organization's name. Archibald MacLeish and Julian Huxley, who would be the first director-general, supported these moves.

It is interesting that the drafters of the UNESCO Constitution understood the word "scientific" and its inclusion in the organization's name as a philosophical rather than a technical move. This move is perhaps best embodied in Julian Huxley's monograph *UNESCO: Its Purpose and Its Philosophy*, which Huxley hoped would embody the organization's sense of purpose through scientific humanism. Huxley's document advanced beliefs in evolution, progress, and the scientific method. In defining UNESCO's program, he noted that science had to be understood in the broadest sense "to cover all the primarily intellectual activities of man, the whole range of knowledge and learning."[6] As detailed later in this chapter and next, UNESCO has held steadfast to this broad sense of purpose in defining the sectoral agendas in the natural sciences as well as in the social and human sciences. Joseph Needham himself headed the first natural sciences division and was personally involved in pushing prominent international and interdisciplinary scientific cooperation programs in UNESCO. Julian Huxley's monograph, however, faced a controversial fate. The Soviet bloc dismissed it as Western propaganda, while many intellectuals within the West viewed it as leaning dangerously close to eugenics and atheism.

A final issue to be resolved in UNESCO's formation was its relationship with the United Nations. UNESCO would be aligned with the Economic and Social Council as a specialized agency of the UN. The UN's incorporation of the International Labour Organization in 1946 served as a model.[7] Articles 57 and 63 of the UN Charter provided the formal framework for incorporation including mutual recognition, participation in meetings and cooperation among the specialized agencies, all of which received budgetary autonomy. Member states thus contributed directly to UNESCO's budget rather than having it sliced directly from the UN system. The association with the UN, however, allows UNESCO to approach its parent and other UN programs and agencies for extra-budgetary resources, which in the 1960s began to rival the regular budget.

Two additional observations help to situate UNESCO's role within the UN system. First, UNESCO has never shied away from defining its objectives broadly, as seen above in the role of science. This leads one observer to note that, "UNESCO is easily the least 'specialized' of the specialized agencies, since its constitutional mandate embraces education, social and natural sciences, culture and communication."[8] James Sewell notes that "UNESCO was born plural."[9] Second, although UNESCO is not a UN-funding agency such as the UNDP, it often comes under pressure, from both within and outside of its ranks, to act like one.[10] It has limited capabilities and resources to fund programs and activities, especially at the level of member states, but as subsequent chapters will show, UNESCO has been asked to implement and fund projects based on the norms it seeks to institutionalize.

Political context for activities

Before describing UNESCO's activities and organization, a brief political context helps to provide a framework for understanding UNESCO functioning. Three themes are traced here: the Cold War, post-colonial politics, and neo-liberal institutionalism. They might oversimplify the situation but are nevertheless useful for locating the constraints upon UNESCO's actions.

UNESCO's Preparatory Committee had barely started to draft the Constitution when the Soviet Union decided not to send representatives. The Soviets would support the moves for the creation of a United Nations but CAME negotiations, falling as they were outside of the UN negotiations at that time, were viewed as Western political propaganda. The first substantive issue to feature these divisions was the US push for freedom of information and media. To be sure, the issue came from the UN, albeit with US pressures. In 1946, the UN General Assembly created the Sub-Commission on Freedom of Information and of the Press (SCFIP) to consider these issues from a human rights perspective. The UN Resolution specifically empowered ECOSOC but UNESCO began to provide its services for SCFIP's deliberations. In 1947, Poland tabled a draft resolution that would make flows of information subject to "friendly international cooperation."[11] Hungary supported Poland and noted that those who believe that wars begin in the minds of men should understand Poland's stance. Poland and Czechoslovakia withdrew from UNESCO in 1947. In 1952, SCFIP was dissolved and the USSR rejoined in 1954 along with Poland and Czechoslovakia. Nevertheless, Cold War politics continued.

A number of Cold War issues revolved around the director-general's office. Luther Evans, an American academic and UNESCO's fourth director-general from 1953–58, was viewed as incredibly efficient but failed to stand up to McCarthyism and the inevitable witch-hunts of staff members at UNESCO. Earlier Jaime Torres-Bodet resigned over UNESCO's budget not getting approved, but it was well-known that he was also not toeing the US line. In 1961, the Soviets protested the election of René Maheu, for them yet another director-general from the Western world. Cold War politics also began to co-mingle with North–South politics as a number of post-colonial developing countries joined UNESCO. The last of the major moves here was the Soviet support for the New World Information and Communication Order at UNESCO during the 1970s and 1980s—criticizing Western domination of information media, content, and flows—that was one of the factors that led to the withdrawal of the United States from UNESCO. More recently, a few whimpers were published in disparate news reports regarding the 2009 election of Irina Bokova, the tenth director-general, critiquing her political lineage (her father was in the Politburo of the Bulgarian Communist Party).

By its twentieth anniversary in 1966, UNESCO's membership had grown to 120 countries from its initial 20 in 1946. The growth in the 1960s was in major part driven by ex-colonial countries. The same United States that had supported the nationalist struggles in these countries would begin to complain of "the tyranny of the majority" in the UN.[12] Early in the 1960s, Director-General René Maheu noted that "operational assistance" to these countries had become a part of UNESCO's activities, which began to draw from the UN Expanded Program of Technical Assistance and the UN Special Fund. Together these UN contributions were part of UNESCO's extra-budgetary resources and a sizable portion of its revenues.[13] UNESCO's

development agenda took shape in the context of Third World advocacy with the formation of organizations such as the Non-Aligned
Movement (NAM) in 1955.

Other developments within the UN system spurred movement in
UNESCO. As discussed in Chapter 5, calls for a New World Information Communication Order (NWICO) in 1976 to correct the information imbalances between the North and South followed the moves
in the UN General Assembly in 1974 for a New International Economic Order with a broader scope. Amadou-Mahatar M'Bow of Senegal
became the seventh director-general of UNESCO. To many at that
time, NWICO and a developing country director-general represented
the new relevance of UNESCO. However, the organization was soon
fraught with charges of inefficiency and corruption. Furthermore, a
series of "Israel resolutions" in the UN and similar moves in UNESCO,
starting from René Maheu's time, sought to equate Zionism with racism.
Cold War politics played into such developments: the Soviet Union
encouraged and supported the Israel resolutions. Henry Kissinger
declared in 1975 that UNESCO and the ILO were now "heavily politicized." In 1976, Israel's foreign minister Abba Eban convened a
Committee Against Further Politicization of UN Agencies. That same
year, Israel secured its place in UNESCO by getting admitted as a
member of the Europe group, after it was voted out of the Arab states
regional group to which it had belonged after a highly politicized
voting procedure. The claims of politicization, inefficiency, and NWICO
advocacy led to US withdrawal from UNESCO in 1985.

UNESCO has emerged over the last two decades as a less controversial and more focused organization. This may be partly due to
the end of the Cold War and the breakup of the Soviet Union, and
perhaps as a ricochet of the charges of inefficiency in the 1980s. The
triumph of neo-liberal institutions and markets worldwide since the
1980s has also weakened the hold of Cold War type ideological battles
and militant developing world advocacy for redistribution of resources.
Instead, UNESCO's programs are now moving toward becoming more
focused and pragmatic. UNESCO is also emerging as an important
node in the UN network. It has secured its place by receiving the
mandate for implementing one of the Millennium Development Goals
for universal primary education in 2002.[14] There is also some backlash
against neo-liberalism in the framing in 2005 of the 2005 Convention
for the Protection and Promotion of the Diversity of Cultural Expressions to counterbalance the World Trade Organization's (WTO) mandate for liberalizing flows of cultural products (see Chapter 4 for
details).[15] However, countries like Canada and France—who provided

leadership for this convention—are firmly within the neo-liberal global order themselves and their moves are viewed more in political than ideological terms. The Convention mandate should be viewed, perhaps, in a more pragmatic context. In terms of other trends within the liberal global economy, it is unclear how UNESCO will be affected by the recent global financial crisis beyond a decrease in its regular and extra-budgetary resources.

UNESCO, of course, did not have to wait until the 1990s to start building its institutions. Throughout its history, the organization's remarkable achievements lie in areas where member states, individuals, and non-governmental organizations have worked together to solve humanity's problems. For every blemish from the Cold War or militant developing country advocacy, UNESCO can point to consensus in scientific cooperation, cultural preservation, and human rights progress.

Purpose, functions, and activities

UNESCO's purpose, functions and activities are well defined in its Constitution, and to its credit the organization has undertaken most of its activities within the mandate of this Constitution. Article 1:1 of its Constitution notes:

> The purpose of the Organization is to contribute to peace and security by promoting collaboration among the nations through education, science and culture in order to further universal respect for justice, for the rule of law and for the human rights and fundamental freedoms which are affirmed for the peoples of the world, without distinction of race, sex, language or religion, by the Charter of the United Nations.

The wording lends weight to the Preamble's quest to sow the seeds of peace and security in the minds of human beings through the spread of education, science and culture. The quest for peace is realized through positive instruments, especially at the psychological level, for diminishing the causes of war through knowledge, cultural understanding, and science. Examples include the education of Palestinian refugee children through UNESCO-UNRWA (United Nations Relief Works Agency) schools beginning in 1949 and its "Culture of Peace" program starting in the 1990s. Peace through negative instruments such as the cessation of hostilities or disarmament is not within the scope of the organization's mandate, although UNESCO in general would lend its weight toward humanitarian intervention in times of war (as in the

UNRWA schools) or scientific cooperation on nuclear matters (as in its help setting up the European laboratory for solid state physics, CERN, on the French-Swiss border near Geneva). Recently UNESCO has entered the arena of post-conflict post-disaster (PCPD) in areas of its competence such as rehabilitating education or maintaining cultural heritage.

UNESCO's philosophy is rooted in humanism and enlightenment: knowledge of others' ways, participation in others' lives and rituals, and exchange and cooperation lead to security and peace. Nevertheless, the belief that people who know each other or are highly educated will always lead peaceful lives is questionable. The Hobbesian belief in human nature points in a different direction. Social scientists proceed cautiously when it comes to analyzing UNESCO's positive peace agenda. Sagarika Dutt provides a literature review of cognitive theories and evidence questioning whether war is only about thoughts and images. He cites Reinhold Niebuhr:

> Ignorance may aggravate fear. But it is not true that knowledge of each other's ways necessarily allays suspicion and mistrust. Some of the most terrible conflicts in history have occurred between neighbors who knew each other quite well, Germany and France for instance.[16]

British academic Richard Hoggart cites Herman Hesse:

> I must confess that I have no faith whatever in the concerted action of intellectuals or in the good will of the "civilized world." The mind cannot be measured in terms of quantity, and whether ten or a hundred "leading lights" appeal to the mighty to do or not to do something, such an appeal is hopeless.[17]

While Herman Hesse would provide a pessimistic view of the kinds of efforts that UNESCO undertakes, he nevertheless concludes his remarks by noting that politicians and policy-makers are too often swayed by the electorate to undertake activities that lead to horrific results. Instead, Hesse enjoins the intellectuals and writers to not play by "their rules" but by upholding truth. UNESCO at its best rises to uphold the truth and at its worst, it caves into pressure from its constituents that dilute its mission.

While the "wars in the minds of men" thesis will remain debatable, UNESCO's mandate in other ways is supplied by its Constitution. Key phrases in Article I:2, clauses a, b, and c, of the Constitution (see Appendix), discussed below provide an understanding of the kinds of activities that UNESCO undertakes to fulfill its mission and purpose.

International agreements

Article I:2a enjoins UNESCO to recommend or craft international agreements. While these international agreements could cover the setting up of a resource center or the undertaking of a study, this section details the legal instruments at UNESCO's disposal. There are three primary types of legal means known as "standard settings" or "normative" instruments. In describing the functions of UNESCO's General Conference, Article IV:B4 of the Constitution distinguishes between conventions and recommendations. Conventions require a two-thirds majority vote in the General Conference, while a simple majority suffices for recommendations. Since the 1990s, the General Conference has tried to move toward consensual decision-making that is becoming the norm in the United Nations. The other instrument used frequently in UNESCO is declarations.

Conventions are legally binding treaties that states adopt and ratify, often through domestic legislation, and which compel them to particular courses of action. The UNESCO secretariat favors implementing norms through conventions because they find the most resonance with member states. The procedure for a convention begins with a formal study of the issue to be governed. The study is then deliberated in the Executive Board, which then sends a proposal to the General Conference. Meanwhile the director-general prepares a report and invites comments and discussion. The 1952 Universal Copyright Convention is an example that arose from detailed studies of comparative copyright laws that led to an international agreement on copyright and provided the most comprehensive instrument for copyright issues; several states adopted its practices until its supersession by the Berne Convention of 1961. The USSR favored UNESCO's Convention over the Berne Convention because the former limited exclusive copyright protection to 25 years, thus curtailing capitalist revenues in its estimate, while the Berne Convention stipulated 50 years.

Recommendations, while voted upon by the General Conference, do not require ratification. They are invitations for member states to take particular courses of action and exhort them to change their domestic practices, laws, or institutions. Chapter 4 discusses the case of the 1989 Recommendation on the Safeguarding of Traditional Culture and Folklore, which created the impetus for and resulted in the 2003 Convention on Intangible Cultural Heritage.

Declarations can be understood as moral suasions or imperatives on important matters. Hence the declaration, endorsed by 40 states and adopted by acclamation at the Second General Conference in Mexico in 1948, titled "Solemn Appeal Against the Idea that Wars Are Inevitable" (see Box 1.1). Declarations may also take the form of charters, such as the "Charter of National Commissions for UNESCO," adopted in 1978.

Article IV, paragraph six of the constitution indicates that member states are to send reports on their compliance with conventions and recommendations. In reality, member states often do not comply, not even when the director-general specifically requests these reports. Nevertheless, the list of conventions, recommendations and declarations provides a veritable catalogue of UNESCO's normative action.[18] UNESCO lists

---

Box 1.1 UNESCO declaration: Solemn Appeal Against the Idea that Wars Are Inevitable

The representatives of Education, Science and Culture, meeting together at Mexico City at the UNESCO General Conference:

AWARE of the responsibilities imposed upon them by the Constitution of the Organisation to further universal respect for justice, for the rule of law, for human rights, and the fundamental freedoms of the peoples of the world, without distinction of race, sex, language or religion;

CONCERNED at the dangers to peace resulting from currents of thought conducive to the idea that another war is inevitable;

TROUBLED by the indifference, resignation and even calm acceptance which such currents of thought meet in certain sections of public opinion;

address a solemn appeal to all who are concerned for the dignity of Man and the future of civilisation, particularly educationalists, scientists, artists, writer and journalists throughout the world;

adjure them to denounce the pernicious idea that war is inevitable;

to act as the mouthpiece of the conscience of the nations, refusing collective suicide;

to combat, by every means in their power, surrender to fear and every form of thought or action which may threaten a just and lasting peace.

(Source: UNESCO document 2C/res.X.3 [1948])

28 conventions, 31 recommendations, and 13 declarations as having been adopted by the end of the 35th General Conference in 2009.[19] For example, Martha Finnemore, using the idea of normative action in a broader sense of prescriptions for behavior (compared to the narrow legal definition used in this sub-section) demonstrates how states have complied, and catalogues evidence showing how ministries of science came about in various countries precisely because of the norms shaped by UNESCO.[20]

Programs

Article I:2b and c suggest programmatic action in the fields of education, culture, and science, while mass communication is mentioned in Article 1:2a itself. UNESCO varies between classifying its agenda as "themes" or as "sectoral programs." Naturally, most of the international agreements mentioned above are also classified and included in these themes or sectors, as well as the initiatives in intellectual cooperation and knowledge creation mentioned later. This sub-section briefly outlines programmatic activities while more detailed descriptions or controversies within these sectors—or, in Richard Hoggart's words, "world-wide parishes" for the assistant directors-general of these sectors[21]—are provided in later chapters:

Education

Education is UNESCO's largest field of action and the reason for the creation of the organization. Over one-fourth of the total regular programs budget and over one-sixth of the organization's total regular budget in 2010–11 is allocated to education (see Table 1.1). Historically, the percentage budget allocations for education were higher. Its staff of 400 is nearly one-fourth of the total staff of the secretariat. Programs in this sector have been aimed at providing universal access, increasing quality of education, and promoting peace and human rights through education. The sector works with education ministries, though its ability to implement specific projects is limited. Nevertheless, it has also set up various regional resource centers and institutes for teacher training and other needs (see below).

Education is broadly defined: one of the first initiatives from this sector launched in the 1940s was "fundamental education" to enable people to lead fuller lives. Nevertheless, the sector could not boast a monumental program to its credit until the launch of the Education for All initiative (EFA) after an inter-agency UN conference in Jomtien, Thailand, in 1990.[22] A follow-up conference in Dakar, Senegal, in 2000

Table 1.1 Unesco biennial budget 2010–2011: regular and extrabudgetary resources (US dollars)

	Regular Budget			Extra-budgetary Resources	Total
	Activities	*Staff*	*Total 35 C/5*		
Part 1: Policy and Direction	23 711 700	20 915 000	44 626 7000	1 437 000	46 063 700
Part II: Programmes and Programme Related Services					
A. Programmes					
Education	56 175 700	62 360 000	118 535 700	62 008 300	180 544 000
Natural Sciences	20 499 600	38 574 400	59 074 000	185 122 100	244 196 100
Of which IOC	3 449 900	6 037 300	9 487 200	8 683 600	18 170 800
Social and Human Sciences	9 671 800	19 982 300	29 654 100	27 024 700	56 678 800
Culture	17 201 000	36 548 700	53 749 700	71 376 700	125 126 400
Of which WHC	4 573 200	7 759 100	12 332 300	34 376 700	46 709 000
Communication & Information	13 108 800	20 049 200	33 158 000	83 323 700	116 481 700
Unesco Institute for Statistics	9 128 600		9 128 600		9 128 600
Field – Management of decentralized programmes	–	56 189 400	56 189 400	1 312 900	57 502 300
Total II.A	125 785 500	233 704 000	359 489 500	430 168 400	789 657 900
Program-related Services	5 070 800	25 897 200	30 968 000	7 809 700	38 777 700
Participation Programme	20 215 500	1 625 700	21 841 200	3 424 900	25 266 100
TOTAL PART II	151 071 800	261 226 900	412 298 700	441 403 000	853 701 700
Part III: Support for Programme Admin.	79 119 100	104 305 100	183 424 200	19 911 400	203 335 600
TOTAL I-III	253 902 600	386 447 000	640 349 600	462 751 400	1 103 101 060
Reserves for reclassifications/merit-based promotion		2,000,000	2,000,000		2,000,000
Part IV: Anticipated Cost Increases	852 700	9 797 700	10 650 400		10 650 400
TOTAL, PARTS I-IV	254 755 300	398 244 700	653 0000 000	462 751 400	1 113 751 460

Source: Unesco, 35 C/5 Draft Programmes and Budget, p. 3.
Available at: unesdoc.unesco.org/images/0018/001811/181173e.pdf Accessed March 11, 2010

integrated a few aspects of EFA into the education-related Millennium Development Goals and the UN appointed UNESCO to be the lead agency in these areas. Over the last 65 years, UNESCO has also opened several centers and institutes for training. For example, in 1951, the establishment of the first international training center in Pátzcuaro, Mexico followed the fundamental education program mentioned above. The center served 16 Latin American countries. A second center was opened in 1953 in Sirs-el-Layyar, Egypt, for Arab countries. The five current global centers and institutes for education include:

- International Bureau of Education (IBE), Geneva
- International Institute for Educational Planning (IIEP), Paris and Buenos Aires
- The UNESCO Institute for Lifelong Learning (UIL), Hamburg
- Institute for Information Technologies in Education (IITE), Moscow
- International Centre for Technical and Vocational Education and Training (UNEVOC), Bonn.

Natural sciences

The "S" almost did not get included in UNESCO's name but now has a staff of 200. Since its inclusion, the sector has tried to balance a broad approach to science, rooted in promoting the role of science and the scientific method that Julian Huxley advocated, with a specific approach geared toward programs and institutions. Even with both in balance, further difficulty lies in matching the science programs with UNESCO's overall mandate of peace and security. UNESCO's uniqueness lies in being the lead UN agency for promoting science, and it has had some considerable success in promoting the cause of science and science ministries worldwide. For example, it persuaded Nigeria in 2006 to commit $5 billion to science.

In terms of programs, UNESCO has focused on natural resources and sustainable development, with a view toward exploring the causes of conflict surrounding natural resource issues. Scientists are in general well-prepared for the former task, but the latter requires an intersectoral approach, which is not one of their strengths. Nevertheless, UNESCO launched its arid zones project to examine deserts and arid zones in 1950 involving 28 disciplines. The agency boasts that it came up with the "sustainable development" label in the 1960s. It has significant comparative advantage in water- and ocean-related issues with global activities such as the International Hydrological Programme (IHP) and the Intergovernmental Oceanographic Commission (IOC). After the 2004 Tsunami, the IOC helped to design the Indian Ocean Tsunami Early

Warning System (IOTWS). The "Man and the Biosphere" program was launched in the early 1970s. A focus on the biosphere and the environment remain important programs. UNESCO also provided scientific advice on the global warming negotiations leading up to Copenhagen in December 2009, and has included programs on natural disasters and conflict management such as Tsunami warning systems. However, the major criticism of this sector is that while it is the lead agency for science in the United Nations, it is relatively unknown among scientists beyond those involved in sustainability and natural resource issues.

Social and human sciences

Social and human sciences have been the most neglected area in UNESCO, with the smallest budget of the five sectors. Nevertheless, the "S" of UNESCO includes both natural sciences, and social and human sciences. The social and human sciences' main activities are either under international agreements (mentioned above) or intellectual cooperation (mentioned below). However, the sector has received increasing attention since the term of Director-General Federico Mayor. Pierre Sané, the former secretary-general of Amnesty International, is the assistant director-general of this sector. Key programs now deal with social transformation, ethics in science, and human rights. The Management of Social Transformations (MOST) program examines social issues including migration, urban growth, and state-formation from international, comparative, and interdisciplinary perspectives. The sector has examined scientific ethics in general and bioethics in particular, as well as morality (always controversial in Anglo-Saxon countries) in the human genome project and genetic research through bodies including the World Commission on the Ethics of Scientific Knowledge and Technology (COMEST), the Intergovernmental Bioethics Committee (IGBC) and the International Bioethics Committee (IBC).

Culture

Most people around the world associate UNESCO with culture through flagship programs such as the UNESCO World Heritage sites, that now number 890. The budget for this sector now comes a close second to that for education. Its World Heritage program now seeks to preserve human creations as well as underwater and natural heritage. Human creations include tangible heritage such as the Sydney Opera House, or intangible heritage embedded in creative processes passed from one generation to the next, such as the art of Maqam singing in Central Asia and the Middle East. Though often critiqued for acting like a global ministry of culture, the sector has nevertheless prioritized the importance of cultural policies in member states and, more recently, creative industries. Director-General Veronese (1958–61) helped to link culture with sources of economic growth, especially through tourism (see Chapter 4). This trend continues, though now it is co-joined with concerns regarding sustainability. More recently the sector has dealt with issues of cultural diversity and preservation by highlighting the importance of developing national capacities for boosting or developing particular types of cultural forms.

Communication and information (C & I)

Although not part of the UNESCO acronym, the sector has featured prominently in UNESCO controversies over the years including over its budget, which is bigger than that of the sciences. Historically, its programs focused on freedom of the media, press, and information flows. In the 1940s these issues were viewed differently in the Eastern bloc, which presented media freedoms in the context of service to state-building efforts. During the 1970s and 1980s, the sector gained prominence with the controversial New World Information and Communication Order (NWICO) debates. At a technical level the sector has generally helped member states develop policy and regulatory capacities for infrastructural diffusion. Lately, it has participated in efforts to bridge the "digital divide" and introduce e-government and furthered the notion of "knowledge societies." Many of its projects focus on community media centers and sustainable technology.

Intersectoral and interdisciplinary programs

Apart from the sectoral themes or efforts, many of UNESCO's programs have been interdisciplinary and intersectoral. In the past 30–40 years, it has designated two such major programs in every five-year budget cycle. The 2006–11 budget cycle has prioritized "Africa" and "gender." The 2001–6 cycle gave impetus to "information and communication technology" and "poverty reduction." The programs tend to be quite broad and intersectoral competition for meager resources tends to be intense, trumping cooperation.

Knowledge creation and diffusion

The moral and ethical force of UNESCO's ideas lies in its power to gather the world's intellectuals and experts in deliberating issues.

Article I, paragraph 2c, provides the mandate and is appropriately titled "Maintain, increase, and diffuse knowledge." Specifically, it goes on to mention dissemination of knowledge through books and art, intellectual exchanges and cooperation, and publications. UNESCO's sectors can each boast several achievements in this arena and the organization is well known for its resource manuals for professionals working around the world in each of the thematic areas. In particular, the work of the UNESCO Institute for Statistics (UIS) is important in collecting and disseminating data on issues that are frequently hard to measure, such as education quality or cultural diversity. A few sectoral highlights are summarized below:

Education: The work of UNESCO institutes in education, mentioned earlier, continues to convene experts and produce reports on topics ranging from the role of education in post-conflict reconstruction to providing teacher training manuals. For example, the sector's *World Education Report* summarizes state-of-the-art thinking and statistical background on the Education for All goals.

Natural Sciences: Bringing expert scientists together to deliberate the role of science is the sector's major strength. The *UNESCO Sourcebook for Science Teaching* is a bestseller with 2 million copies printed. It explains the importance of science and its foundational concepts in simple terms.

Social and Human Sciences: A few of the greatest issues confronting humanity, from racism to human rights to social transformations, have been deliberated and debated at UNESCO. Claude Lévi-Strauss' seminal scholarship on racism arose from his work at UNESCO. Of particular importance for this sector is its role in helping start many international social science associations in various disciplines. It also publishes the *International Social Science Journal*.

Culture: UNESCO helped to start the International Council of Museums, which remains the authoritative organization for curation and museology. It created an epistemic movement for bringing attention to neglected histories of regions and issues through works such as the monumental *General History of Africa* and *History of Mankind: Scientific and Cultural Development*. Famous reports from this sector include *Our Creative Diversity* (1995), which linked socio-economic development to culture and also contributed to the momentum for UNESCO's current attention given to cultural diversity. Two *World Culture Reports* in 1998 and 2000 helped to do the same.

Communication and Information: Wilbur Scharmm's tome *Mass Media and National Development*, still used in policy and academic work worldwide, helped to create the momentum for telecommunications and media infrastructures. During the NWICO era, the sector turned out voluminous reports, both quantitative and qualitative, on information flows through various media. These reports showed how Western media firms and houses dominated most flows from the North to the South (see Chapter 5).

UNESCO's contribution to problem solving and its creation of a store of knowledge cannot be easily dismissed. Nevertheless, the impact of many of these intellectual ventures remains uncertain. Certainly, the gathering of the world's intellectuals in various disciplines has created a sense of camaraderie among them but has also led to the impression that UNESCO is an elitist academic institution. The reports produced have definitely led to the creation of international agreements and programs, but UNESCO has limited resources to venture effectively into each of the broad programs of action that it deliberates.

The organization

The idealism enshrined in UNESCO's Constitution must be realized through its organizational parts and design: nearly 200 member states, a secretariat varying historically between 2 and 3,000, and a repository for the world's intellectuals and civil society organizations. While in 1990, UNESCO had a staff of around 2,700, a decade later it had come down to around 2,100 as the organization adjusted to budget cuts from the US exit in 1984. Director-General Matsuura is credited with reducing the ratio of Paris versus field offices staff from 3:1 to 2:1 now. In 2010 there were 58 field offices. UNESCO's combined regular and extra-budgetary resources amount to only a billion dollars biennially, less than the budget for a large research university in the United States.

Member states

In 1960 UNESCO had 99 members. In 1980, there were 153. As of January 2010, there were 193 member states and 7 associate members in UNESCO. Associate members include territories such as Macao or the Cayman Islands that do not conduct their own external relations (Table 1.2). There were surges in membership in the late 1950s and 1960s with the post-colonial states and again in the 1990s with the break up of the Soviet Union and other states in Eastern Europe.

UNESCO classifies its states into five regional groups: Africa, Arab states, Asia and the Pacific, Europe and North America, and Latin America and the Caribbean. Regional politics often rise to the top of UNESCO's agenda, most recently in the election of the tenth director-general, Irina Bokova, who took over on 15 November 2009. Bokova

Table 1.2 Total member states and executive board members

Year	Member states	Executive board members
1946	28	18
1950	59	18
1960	99	24
1970	125	34
1980	153	51
1990	161	51
2000	188	58
2010	193	58

Source: unesco.org

narrowly defeated Egypt's minister of culture, Farouk Hosny, who would have been the first DG from an Arab state. Hosny was expected to win, but he lost support when discussion erupted among prominent intellectuals and member states over anti-Semitic comments Hosny had made. Earlier, in November 1974, during the third of the so-called Israel resolutions (as they came to be known), it became impossible for Israel to remain a member of the Arab states group. Israel retained its membership by becoming inducted into the Europe group. The director-general's elections and, historically, Israel's membership have featured some colorful discussions at UNESCO.

Regional groupings among the member states are subject to global shifts in politics. During the Cold War, great power rivalries shaped many deliberations. Richard Hoggart makes some of his sharpest observations on the behavior of the Soviets and those of the Chinese in his witty book on UNESCO:

> One is aware that they have been trained to make political capital out of each issue. They will side with the Arab States in accusing Israel of blatant offences against human rights; they will join with the new nations in any anti-colonialist resolution; they will take every opportunity to criticize the USA as a capitalist super-state. This last procedure has been inhibited since the entry of mainland China, whose representatives insert in every speech a fierce reference to "the hegemony of the superpowers, the USSR and the USA."[23]

Most member states maintain permanent delegations to UNESCO, usually headed by an ambassador. As of January 2010, 182 member states, 4 observers, and 9 intergovernmental organizations maintained permanent missions to UNESCO. Permanent delegations often get their instructions from a ministry designated by their home government or capital. The lead ministry most commonly affiliated with UNESCO is education followed by foreign affairs. In a few cases culture, sports or tourism are designated. Interestingly, developing countries tend to designate education as their lead ministry responsible to UNESCO, whereas developed countries tend to designate their ministry of foreign affairs. The United Kingdom designates the secretary of state for international development. UNESCO covers several issues that span various ministries in any country and thus the lead ministry may or may not be able to coordinate the inter-ministerial efforts. However, UNESCO is unique in the UN family in providing for National Commissions. Article VII of UNESCO's Constitution provides for the appointment of National Commissions for UNESCO in an advisory capacity:

> Each Member State shall make such arrangements as suit its particular conditions for the purpose of associating its principal bodies interested in educational, scientific and cultural matters with the work of the Organization, preferably by the formation of a National Commission broadly representative of the government and such bodies.

Table 1.3 details the ministries responsible for relations with UNESCO.

The idea of the National Commissions reflects the French push for a non-governmental organization at the CAME negotiations. National Commissions therefore represent a compromise of sorts to allow civil society to play a role. In the case of the United States, a 100-member National Commission is established under the Federal Advisory Committee Act of 1972 and includes not more than 60 NGO members and 40 "outstanding members" which may include not more than 10 members from federal government, not more than 15 members from state and local government, and not more than 15 at-large members.[24]

All 193 members and three of the associate members (Aruba, British Virgin Islands, and Netherlands Antilles) have established National Commissions. Their primary role is advisory but they also connect national missions to important organizations and institutions within the country of origin. In rare cases, the work of the UNESCO commissions overlaps or even supersedes that of the permanent delegations. However, the degree of effectiveness of UNESCO National Commissions is limited and varies according to their organizational strength and national resources. Most National Commissions toe the home government's line; there are only a few instances of National Commissions taking an independent stance. Furthermore, the French National Commission for UNESCO has been a particularly effective one in an advisory capacity to the government's policy-making for UNESCO.

Table 1.3 Ministries responsible for relations with UNESCO

Regions/ ministries	Africa	Arab states	Asia and the Pacific	Europe and North America	Latin America and Caribbean
Education/ teaching/ research	25	16	23	11	27
Culture		1		5	1
Technology/ science/ information			1		1
Foreign affairs		1	16	32	8
Special ministry for UNESCO/ special state dignitary			4	1	1
Human resources development			1		
International development				1	
No minister				1	

Source: unesco.org (calculated from "Member States Ministries," available at: http://portal.unesco.org/en/ev.php-URL_ID=33357&URL_DO=DO_TOPIC& URL_SECTION=201.html).

General Conference

The General Conference, meeting every two years, comprises of representatives of the member states. It is the chief decision-making body of UNESCO and sets the programmatic and budgetary agendas for the organization. The first General Conference of UNESCO met in November–December 1946 at the Sorbonne in Paris. The second General Conference in 1947 met in Mexico City. After the construction of the main UNESCO headquarters building in 1958 at Place de Fontenoy in Paris, the General Conference has generally met in Paris except for a few sessions such as the 19th Session in Nairobi (1976) and the 21st Session in Belgrade (1980). The Constitution also allows for extraordinary sessions of the General Conference, four of which have been held so far in Paris (1948, 1953, 1973 and 1982).

The General Conference meets in plenary sessions to deliberate and vote upon matters such as budget, director-general's appointment and those of the Executive Board (see below), and passing of draft resolutions (99 presented at the 35th General Conference in 2009). Four committees assist its work: General, Credentials, Nominations, and Legal. Beyond the plenary and the committees, the other bodies of the General Conference are the commissions for budget, administration, and for each of the five UNESCO sectors. Other committees and commissions are appointed as necessary.

Each member state has one vote. Normative decisions in UNESCO, as in other UN bodies, are now generally made by consensus. Despite this move, most decisions only require a simple majority, while issues such as induction of members and observers require a two-thirds majority. As with other international organizations, multilateral and bilateral efforts at global meetings often take the shape of "corridor diplomacy." The working languages of the General Conference are Arabic, Chinese, English, French, Spanish, and Russian. The translation and interpretation work is time-consuming and draws upon enormous resources.

Executive Board

The Executive Board, representative of UNESCO member states, meets every six months and is one of the three constitutional bodies of the organization along with the General Conference and the secretariat. The General Conference elects the 58 members for four-year terms in office. Over the years the number of members and terms in office have changed. When UNESCO began, the Board had 18 members elected for three years (see Table 1.2). The Executive Board meets every six months or four times during the biennium between the General Conferences. Its function is best described as both preparing the agenda for the General Conference and implementing the latter's decisions.

The Executive Board is the de facto governing body of UNESCO. It nominates the director-general, its decisions guide the overall agenda of the General Conference, and its meetings shape the implementation of the programs and the allocations of the budget. The role of the Executive Board is crucial in reaching consensus at the General Conference. Once elected to the Board, the member states appoint a representative to the Executive Board. The appointee is supposed to then represent the geographical and cultural diversity of the region s/he has been elected to represent. In practice, though, the Executive Board members' interests are strongly tied to their own nation-states.

The Secretariat

The hub of UNESCO's activities, the 2,100 person secretariat comprises the international civil service that must implement the organization's mandate. There were nearly 4,000 staff members in 1980 before the exit of the United States and United Kingdom produced a budget crisis. Half the secretariat staff is located in Paris and the rest in the 58 field offices spread throughout the world. UNESCO's multinational workforce comes from nearly 170 of its member states. Apart from the education institutes mentioned above, UNESCO also maintains the Institute for Water Education in Delft, Netherlands, and a Centre for Theoretical Physics in Trieste, Italy. Another important body is the UNESCO Institute for Statistics in Montreal, established in July 1999 to enhance the statistical capabilities of the secretariat.

The selection of the staff is a complicated process requiring geographic and cultural diversity, taking into account the sensitivities of the member states, and due regard for their competence and skill sets. Staff is divided into general service and professional, with the latter's categories ranging from P1 to P5. A P5 carries diplomatic privileges, thus becoming a P5 is a career goal. After achieving this, the next step is to become director. The pressures from both within and from member states for staff to be hired, and promoted to higher ranks, have resulted in a great deal of politicization through UNESCO's history. Along with this politicization, the incompetence of the secretariat staff and nepotism in hiring practices were often mentioned in the 1970s and 1980s. A US General Accounting Office audit in 1984 found widespread cronyism, inflation of salaries, and a general opaqueness regarding salary structures.[25] Nearly 60 percent of the organization's regular budget is allocated toward maintaining staff salaries.

Richard Hoggart is especially critical of the secretariat staff as he observed them from his position as Assistant Director-General of Planning.[26] He found them to be variously incompetent, sensitive, intelligent, slothful, mealy-mouthed, and timid. Only around 40 people or so carried out the brunt of the organization's work: "This is a small group and interestingly, they are known to most members of the secretariat, even to those who try to dismiss their achievements."[27] Thus, there are a number of challenges to running the secretariat, including how to divide the work of UNESCO in various divisions and the challenge of recruiting a competent staff.

As presently organized, an Associate Director-General (ADG) supervises each of UNESCO's sectors. Each sector features various divisions, usually headed by a director. Apart from the Office of the Director-General, two other offices are important for steering the entire organization. These are: the Bureau of Strategic Planning, which sets the overall agenda of the organization; and the Bureau of Budget (see Figure 1.2). As the sectors have become important, each has been headed by an ADG, rather than a director as was the case when UNESCO was founded. As originally organized in 1946 (Figure 1.1), each of the three ADGs were to look after several sectors. Over time, the sectors began to take on distinct identities and were headed by directors who answered to one of the three ADGs. By 1990, the sectors were headed by an ADG answerable to a deputy director-general of programs. The other DDG was to be responsible for management, which included

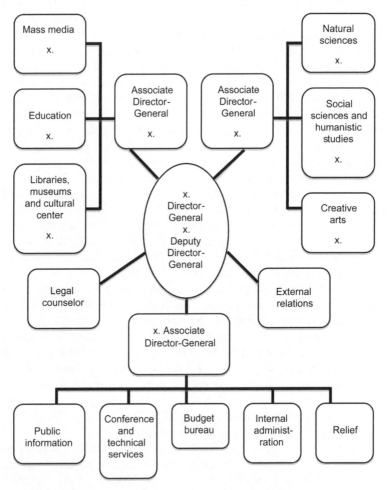

Figure 1.1 Proposed organization of UNESCO secretariat in 1946
Note: x = Cabinet of 11 top people
Source: Adapted from UNESCO archives, Organizational Charts www.unesco.org/archives/charts.htm

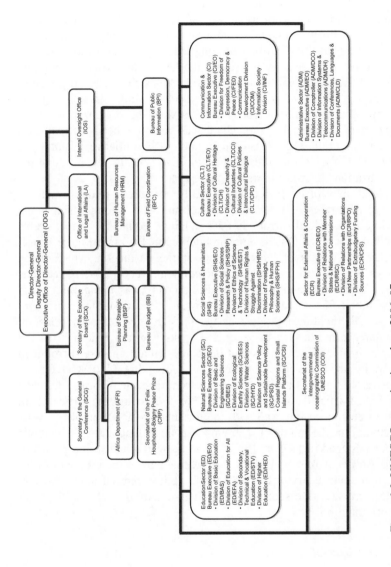

Figure 1.2 UNESCO organization chart 2006–07

personnel, planning and budgetary matters. Unofficially, the five major divisions in UNESCO are identified as "sectors" although officially UNESCO calls them themes or programs.

One of the primary achievements of the ninth director-general, Koïchiro Matsuura, was organizational reforms. Of these, cutting the number of directors by half, from a high of 200, stands out. The field offices were cut from 79 to 58, although the organization was otherwise decentralized by steadily increasing the field office posts. An internal oversight report submitted in January 2009 described several priorities in hiring, which included hiring competent staff, streamlining the hiring process, and synchronizing hires with the organization's strategic plans.[28] While the staff challenges have not been met, officials in general credit DG Matsuura for taking the initiative in cutting a great deal of nepotism, introducing transparency, and streamlining the organizations to speak to its strategic goals.[29]

No account of the secretariat would be complete without describing the various types of UNESCO symbolism, chief among which is the architecture and art surrounding its buildings. Perhaps the most visible symbol of UNESCO is its emblem adopted in 1954 (see Figure I.1). It evokes the temple of Pallas Athena at the Parthenon, which today serves as a historic symbol of democracy and good governance. The main Y-shaped building at Place de Fontenoy was inaugurated on 5 November 1958, and was conceived by an international team of architects. This building is known as the three-pointed star. The General Conference meets in a building that looks like and is known as the Accordion. UNESCO halls and buildings contain and are surrounded by major art works either donated to or acquired by UNESCO. One of these is the Square of Tolerance, a gift from the state of Israel, designed by Israeli artist Dani Karavan in 1996. The square comprises of an olive tree and a stone wall with the first line of the Preamble on wars beginning in the minds of men engraved in 10 languages. A symbolic globe designed in 1995 by the Danish engineer, scientist and professor Erik Reitzel evokes the UN logo. It became part of the installations for the 50th anniversary of UNESCO. Erik Reitzel himself notes that UN delegates may have succeeded in doing something that the Tower of Babel could not.[30]

Director-General

The job of the DG of UNESCO is much like that of a university president in the United States. First, this person heads a deeply philosophical, idealistic, and self-consciously intellectual enterprise even if the

Figure 1.3 The Square of Tolerance designed by Dani Karavan
Photo Source: Claude, Michel

Figure 1.4 UNESCO Symbolic Globe designed by Erik Reitzel
Photo Source: Burke, Niamh

bureaucrats themselves do not deliver on these aims (much like professors who can't teach or publish but talk a good game). Second, this
person is most responsible for the image of the organization and the
way that others perceive it. This includes being able to resist the most
obvious political pressures and maintaining the dignity of an office that
supervises a multinational workforce. Third, perhaps most importantly,
the DG must be a skilled bureaucratic leader, able to deal with the
rivalries within and across sectors and divisions, and able to pull together
the entire enterprise on interdisciplinary issues.

Historically, the various directors-general at UNESCO have delivered
well on one or the other of the organization's goals (see Table 1.4 for the
list of directors-general and their tenure). Several of them are known
for their charisma and idealism but were frustrated by the bureaucratic
and administrative responsibilities of their position: Julian Huxley, Jaime
Torres, and Federico Mayor. Practical and efficient DGs have found it
hard to ward off political pressures: Luther Evans could not face up to
McCarthyism, and Amadou-Mahater M'Bow, apart from nepotism,
caved into the Soviet/Arab bloc. Federico Mayor had a tempestuous
relationship with the Executive Board and found it hard to translate
his intellectual depth and charisma into getting the member states to

Table 1.4 UNESCO Directors-General

	Directors-General	Country	Tenure
1.	Julian Huxley 1887–1975	United Kingdom	1946–1948
2.	Jaime Torres Bodet 1902–1974	Mexico	1948–1952
3.	John W. Taylor 1906–2001	United States	1952–1953
4.	Luther Evans 1902–1981	United States	1953–1958
5.	Vittorino Veronese 1910–1986	Italy	1958–1961
6.	René Maheu 1905–1975	France	1961–1974
7.	Amadou-Mahtar M'Bow 1921–	Senegal	1974–1987
8.	Federico Mayor 1934–	Spain	1987–1999
9.	Koïchiro Matsuura 1937	Japan	1999–2009
10.	Irina Bokova 1952	Bulgaria	2009–

support his programs. DGs such as Vittorio Veronese and Koïchiro Matsuura were skilled diplomats but remained focused on administration. Interestingly, both pushed forward particular agendas of their own: Veronese focused on cultural heritage with the Nubia campaign in Egypt, and Matsuura pushed forward the Convention on Intangible Cultural Heritage (see Chapter 4 for details on both). René Maheu combined the qualities of administration with an intense philosophical zeal and was apt at delivering intellectual lectures to his staff. Despite his authoritarian personality and narcissism, he was re-elected for a second term.

Koïchiro Matsuura's tenure will have an indelible impact on getting the organization focused on practical details of house cleaning. After the departure of the United States and the United Kingdom, UNESCO's image had suffered. Federico Mayor was elected as a "Western" leader to re-balance the organization after M'Bow's director-generalship. However, Mayor is often described as an ivory tower intellectual by those who worked with him at UNESCO. "In Mayor we had esoteric work but without a client or a customer."[31] DG Matsuura made incredible strides toward restoring UNESCO's image but others feel that he was much better at internal house cleaning than at providing global leadership for the organization. However, one senior staff member described him as "intelligent, articulate, smart, very decent, hardworking, and with a good CV."[32]

Despite the fraught election and close contest between Bulgarian Irina Bokova and Egyptian Farouk Hosny, the international community closely avoided a reversion to a visible politicization of the agency.[33] Bokova, the former Bulgarian ambassador to France, may have had the added advantage of being familiar with the inner workings of UNESCO. Like Veronese and Matsuura, she comes from a career in international diplomacy. In interviews and speeches, she avoids the high idealism of the 1960s and 1970s and instead focuses on UNESCO's sectoral priorities and lack of resources.[34]

Strategy and budget

Over its history, UNESCO's challenge has been to maintain coherence between its broad idealism and the implementation of its programs with a limited budget. DG Jaime Torres resigned in 1952 because the General Conference did not sanction his requested appropriation. Another challenge is strategy formulation and choosing among the varieties of program that can span UNESCO's mandate. From the mid-1950s to the late 1960s, UNESCO prioritized its programs through a major projects approach. While the 1950 General Conference had outlined 10 major projects, only three were prioritized between 1957 and 1966, including a project on East–West cultural values, a primary education project in Latin America, and the interdisciplinary Arid Zones Major Project (the latter two were referred to earlier in this chapter). Since the 15th session of the General Conference in 1968, the emphasis began to shift toward preparing plans for a middle term spanning three biennia. The Medium-Term Planning documents have come to be known as C/4 and the first was prepared for the 1977–82 period and approved at the 1976 General Conference. No budget numbers are given for the C/4 document. The 1984–89 Medium Term Plan notes 13 major programs, an approach that harks back to the major projects focus of the 1950s. Since 2000, DG Matsuura streamlined the process of C/4 preparation by establishing the Bureau of Strategic Planning. The Bureau of Strategic Planning works with the Bureau of Budget to prepare the biennial Program and Budget of the Organization, known as C/5. Nevertheless, one staffer notes that there is "no parallel between C/4 and C/5."[35] The C/5 allocations feature the most intense inter-sectoral and member state bargaining, and other battles for budget allocations: "implicit bargaining rather than the slash and burn [of efficient business organizations] decides budgetary priorities." "There are five mini organizations. It's hard to get priority vertically [within a sector]. It's extremely difficult across cultures horizontally."[36] DG Mayor tried horizontal task teams to induce cooperation but the initiative was unsuccessful. In an early speech in 2000 to the Executive Board, DG Matsuura acknowledged this problem in straightforward terms:

> If UNESCO's "comparative advantage"—much of which stems from its unique combination of competencies—is to be fully exploited, the nonsense of "turf battle" has to give way to house-wide team play. The imperative of intersectoral cooperation is being written into the job descriptions of the new program sector ADGs as a major responsibility.[37]

Table 1.1 above provides a summary of the UNESCO Draft Budget for the 2010–11 period, submitted to the 35th General Conference in October 2009. The total regular budget for the organization is $653 million, of which $359 million goes to the five sectors, the UNESCO Institute for Statistics, and the field offices. Of the $359 million, the education sector receives 33 percent, natural sciences 16 percent, social and human sciences 8 percent, culture 15 percent, and communication and information sector 9 percent. Extra-budgetary resources have supplemented UNESCO's regular budget since its inception. Most of these extra-budgetary resources have come from the European Commission,

UN funding agencies such as UNDP and UNICEF, and the multilateral development banks. Such funding has also tugged at UNESCO's mandate for being a specialized agency of the UN shaping global norms rather than being a funding agency or being a development organization. On the other hand, officials note that a few external donors are more likely to impose strict monitoring and evaluation standards, than UNESCO's in-house processes.

The 2010–11 budget draws upon $463 million of extra-budgetary resources, nearly 41 percent of the total $1.1 billion budget for UNESCO. More recently, UNESCO has also begun to partner with private organizations including foundations, businesses, and NGOs. This reflects moves within the entire UN system toward the so-called "global compact" with businesses and non-governmental organizations announced by UN secretary-general Kofi Annan. For example, the Observatory for Cultural Policies in Africa developed through a partnership with the African Union and the Ford Foundation.[38] The L'Oreal-UNESCO program for "Women in Science" is assisting in implementing the third Millennium Development Goal of gender equity. The shift toward private partnerships also reflects the global trend toward private foundations such as the Bill and Melinda Gates Foundation.

In the regular budget, the dues for member states are assessed according to population size and per capita income. The scale follows United Nations standards set by the General Assembly. The minimum contribution is 0.001 percent of the budget and the upper limit is 25 percent, paid historically by the United States and now also by Japan. Around 40 least-developed countries pay the minimum assessment. The exit of United States, United Kingdom, and Singapore in 1984 led to a 30 percent reduction in the budget. Table 1.5 provides a comparison of assessed contributions from member states for UN specialized agencies on an annual basis.

Budget misallocations and the lack of audits were among the reasons that the United States left the organization. Especially in Koïchiro Matsuura's tenure and with the re-entry of the United States to the organization, several steps have been taken to shore up the finances and strategy. The coordination between the bureaus of Budget and Strategic Planning is one such move. An important maneuver to track expenditures and align them with program goals is the implementation of the results-based management approach in the UN system as a whole. Within UNESCO, one aspect of RBM is the implementation of the SISTER online mechanism. It stands for System of Information on Strategies, Tasks and the Evaluation of Results. Its function is to rationalize program goals with allocations and expenditures using RBM. DG Matsuura also

Table 1.5 Assessed contributions to UN specialized agencies: 1971–2009

Year	FAO	ILO	UNESCO	UNIDO	WHO	ICAO	IMO	ITU	UPU	WIPO	WMO	IAEA	TOTAL
1971	36	31	45		75	8	2	8	2	3	4	14	228
1980	139	105	152		214	21	10	44	10	17	17	81	810
1990	278	165	182	94	307	34	23	84	19	19	35	155	1395
2000	322	234	272	66	421	49	30	84	21	11	39	217	1766
2009	469	321	316	113	479	64	50	103	31	16	56	295	2313

Source: Klaus Hüffner, "Assessed Contributions to UN Specialized Agencies," Global Policy Forum (available at: http://www.glob alpolicy.org/un-finance/tables-and-charts-on-un-finance/the-financing-of-the-un-programmes-funds-and-specialized-agencies.html).

established the Internal Oversight Service for audits and monitoring of UNESCO expenditures. Nevertheless, even during Matsuura's tenure, there were prominent scandals and issues about budget misallocations as pointed out in successive audits. Even though the United States has been one of the most vocal in its critique of UNESCO planning and budgeting, the departure of Peter Smith as ADG Education in June 2006 showed that the country's nationals were not themselves immune from corruption. A former Congressman, Peter Smith was accused of nepotism in the awarding of lucrative education consulting contracts.

Intellectuals, experts, and NGOs

As an organization that prides itself as the intellectual and philosophical think-tank of UN organizations, UNESCO furnishes this claim with a network of intellectuals and links to civil society organizations, both transnational and domestic. UNESCO proclaims on its website, "Relations between UNESCO and NGOs are essentially intellectual and moral."[39] In practice, its ties can be intellectual, moral, administrative, expertise-driven, and arise from operational considerations. UNESCO's establishment was also part of the recognition during the creation of the United Nations system, especially with its Economic and Social Council (ECOSOC), that civil society organizations are a key part of the global governance architecture.[40]

Intellectuals and experts play various roles in the myriad consultative committees, commissions, and expert groups at UNESCO. There are also those moments when world-renowned intellectuals take to the podium at UNESCO's deliberations. That is the organization's finest hour, giving a sense of the collective humanity as one being striving for peace. *Reflections of Our Age* documents the speeches given by the world's intellectuals at the first General Conference in 1946 and serves as a poignant reminder of UNESCO's role and function in advancing world peace.[41] Jean-Paul Sartre's words closing his lecture in "The Responsibility of the Writer" are prophetic:

> It is quite possible that the war we are trying to avoid will come. It is quite possible that we won't get a hearing. What we must avoid, we writers, is allowing our responsibility to be changed by guilt, so that fifty years hence it may be said of us: "They saw the greatest world catastrophe coming and they kept silent."[42]

While intellectuals and experts provide input for UNESCO's proceedings, it is UNESCO's relations with NGOs that make up the bulk of its operational relations outside of dealings with governmental organizations and delegates. UNESCO's Constitution supplies the mandate. Article XI on "Relations with other specialized international organizations and agencies" states in paragraph 4:

> The United Nations Educational, Scientific and Cultural Organization may make suitable arrangements for consultation and cooperation with non-governmental international organizations concerned with matters within its competence, and may invite them to undertake specific tasks. Such cooperation may also include appropriate participation by representatives of such organizations on advisory committees set up by the General Conference.

UNESCO has distinguished between *formal relations* and *operational relations* with NGOs since 1995, when elaborate directives tried to institute reforms into this aspect of UNESCO's functioning, which had been critiqued for being politicized and non-transparent. The reforms especially enabled UNESCO to recognize intra-national NGOs and not just international ones. The induction of NGOs falls in the purview of the Committee on Non-governmental Organizations of the Executive Board. *Formal relations*, that may take the form of *formal associate relations* or *formal consultative relations*, allow UNESCO to link with international NGOs, around 330 in 2010, that are recognized experts in their fields of activity. *Operational relations* allow UNESCO to link with domestic and international NGOs in the implementation of its programs. They are entitled to funding and contracts with UNESCO.

Kerstin Martens provides a three-fold classification of the types of affiliation that UNESCO has fostered with NGOs.[43] First, UNESCO created nearly 25 NGOs itself up until 1965 to assist with its mandate. This includes the International Council of Museums (ICOM) created in 1946. Second, UNESCO provided funding to various NGOs to implement its programs. Third, UNESCO favors creating NGOs in specific issues as opposed to playing a direct role itself. Martens provides the example of the World Wildlife Fund founded with UNESCO assistance in 1961. She notes that the number of NGOs recognized at UNESCO increased from 187 in 1961 to 588 in 1995 when the new directives for reform were introduced. The directives both reduced the number of recognized NGOs while also enabling UNESCO to collaborate with or delegate its work to domestic NGOs though *operational relations*.

Beyond intellectuals, experts, and NGOs, UNESCO also maintains a network of affiliations through various means. UNESCO associations, centers and clubs in various countries allow civil society participants to keep abreast with and maintain ties with UNESCO. Since 1951, the organization has also implemented the Associated Schools Project (ASPNet) that links it with more than 8,500 schools in 179 countries. In higher education, UNESCO's 26th General Conference in 1992 established the Unitwin (university twinning) and networking program. The Unitwin/UNESCO Chairs program is responsible for advancing research, collaboration, and learning networks among institutes for higher learning. In 2010, there were 653 UNESCO Chairs and 62 Unitwin networks involving 770 institutions of higher education in 126 countries covering 70 disciplines. Finally, UNESCO maintains a vast network of luminaries who serve as goodwill ambassadors or spokespersons for the organization. The current list of ambassadors includes the soprano Montserrat Caballé, and the human rights activists Rigobertu Menchu and Nelson Mandela.[44]

Conclusion

There is no doubt that despite the many critiques of UNESCO, the organization can still claim for itself the mantle of global intellectual and philosophical leadership. In an otherwise critical review of UNESCO's ponderous and convoluted inner functioning, Richard Hoggart writes:

> In spite of all such disappointments, there are occasionally moments which remind one dramatically what UNESCO is about. I remember Pablo Neruda, in poor health and only a few months from death, standing before the Plenary Meeting of the General Conference and reminding the delegates about UNESCO's fundamental commitment to the poor and deprived of the world, to them as whole human beings not simply as units who have to be made literate and given more money. It was as if the poor of his native Chile, of all Latin America, of the whole world, walked sadly and in silent reproof through that elegant hall, evoked by Neruda's passion and poetry.[45]

This sense of purpose often gets derailed in UNESCO as it chugs along through global power politics, internal rivalries, budgetary battles, and programming priorities. On the more positive side, UNESCO can boast of seminal contributions to global governance through its international conventions, and several well-known programs and institutes. Chapters 2–5 detail the contributions of UNESCO in its five sectors and the controversies and debates these sectors have engendered.

2 Prioritizing education

Education comes before anything else at UNESCO. The negotiations that led to UNESCO initially brought together the Conference of Allied Ministers in Education (CAME). Education informed the utopian foundations of the organization: it would be the corrective in "the minds of men" before they proceed anywhere. Whether education was to be understood as a human right or a form of pedagogy, it would elevate human beings above ignorance. After noting that "defences of peace" are to be constructed in the minds of human beings, the Preamble continues: "that ignorance of each other's ways and lives has been common cause, throughout the history of mankind, of that suspicion and mistrust between the peoples of the world through which their differences have all too often broken into war." The education sector has historically dominated at UNESCO. It currently makes up nearly one-third of the total regular budget for programs (Table 1.1) and one-fifth of the total staff.

Education is central to the humanistic philosophy that guided UNESCO's charter. UNESCO's International Commission for Education in the 21st Century poignantly termed its report *Learning: The Treasure Within* and begins with the following words: "In confronting the many challenges that the future holds in store, humankind sees in education an indispensable asset in its attempt to attain the ideals of peace, freedom and social justice."[1] The archives at UNESCO are replete with documents and speeches locating in education the rationale for the entire organization. In 1945, UNESCO's Preamble also steered the organization to "full and equal opportunities for education for all."

Education also remains the Achilles heel of the organization. If the organization's philosophy and charter are linked to education, then how are these goals to be translated into viable courses of action? In an organization divided into five sectors, can a sector devoted to education speak to the emphasis given to education in the organization's preamble? What if the education sector begins to dominate, materially and organizationally, other sectors in UNESCO? The tensions between education as the guiding philosophy of the organization and education as a sectoral priority have not been resolved easily at UNESCO. For example, a recent intellectual history of the organization notes that by the 1960s, "little by little, a clearer awareness of the immensity and difficulty of the task of coordinating education on a worldwide scale is growing." This history notes that in the 1990s "this tension between the desired ideal and the practical realisation is emblematic of the shaping of humanity." Later, foreshadowing the historical weakness of the education sector, the author notes: "There is nothing worse than hopes that have been dashed. In proclaiming major objectives attainable in the near future, in mobilizing support, one obviously runs the risk of provoking despair and bitterness if the expected results fail to materialize."[2]

UNESCO is currently implementing the Education for All (EFA) initiative that was originally drawn up at the World Conference on Education for All at Jomtien, Thailand, in 1990. UNESCO had always pursued "education for all," an objective which is mentioned in its Preamble; now the initiative itself took on this name. In the four and a half decades prior to Jomtien, and arguably in the decade following Jomtien, UNESCO propounded ideas and goals that were not always translated into practice. The education sector carved out the biggest slice of UNESCO's regular budget and at nearly 400 staff members in 2000, it continued to be the biggest sector in the organization. Nevertheless, perhaps because the task of educating humanity is not simple, the education sector cannot point toward any significant achievement. It would be perhaps easier for it to take ownership of being the primary UN specialized agency in education, but it almost had this mandate "stolen," starting in the late 1960s, by UNICEF and the World Bank, organizations that began to lay out impressive programs in education. It was perhaps this competition that led UNESCO to begin to reformulate its education agenda for Jomtien in the 1980s, but it took another World Education Forum in Dakar, Senegal, in 2000 for UNESCO to pinpoint specific goals that could be realistically achieved and monitored.

Given the context above, this chapter describes the thinking regarding education in four parts. The first section takes up the normative ideas that have both shaped UNESCO's education endeavors and in turn been shaped by them. The second section describes the mostly lackadaisical initiatives in education until 1990. The third section describes the prioritization of education at Jomtien and the decade that followed. The final section takes up the renewed emphasis on education, as linked with other UN goals and global funding mechanisms, and the involvement of both inter-governmental and non-governmental endeavors that may be making a difference in the field of education.

The right to education

From its early days, UNESCO has interpreted its mandate for education not just in terms of its Preamble and Constitution but also in the context of international legal instruments sanctioning a right to education for all human beings. This context pervades UNESCO's emphasis on universal education and guides the organization's work in the drafting of its own normative instruments.

One of the foundational principles to arise from the United Nations is the language of universalism including the ideas of universal human rights. In a recent volume noting 11 UN ideas that changed the world, the idea of universal rights is listed as the first.[3] Until the Universal Declaration of Human Rights (see Box 2.1), rights had been jurisdictionally confined even while espousing cosmopolitan aspirations, such as Thomas Paine's 1791 defense of the French Revolution in the *Rights of Man*. The 1948 Universal Declaration of Human Rights (UDHR) projected the notion of human rights to a global scale and

---

Box 2.1 The Universal Declaration of Human Rights

Preamble

Whereas recognition of the inherent dignity and of the equal and inalienable rights of all members of the human family is the foundation of freedom, justice and peace in the world ...

Article 1

All human beings are born free and equal in dignity and rights. They are endowed with reason and conscience and should act towards one another in a spirit of brotherhood.

Article 2

Everyone is entitled to all the rights and freedoms set forth in this Declaration, without distinction of any kind, such as race, colour, sex, language, religion, political or other opinion, national or social origin, property, birth or other status. Furthermore, no distinction shall be made on the basis of the political, jurisdictional or international status of the country or territory to which a person belongs, whether it be independent, trust, non-self-governing or under any other limitation of sovereignty.

Article 26

1. Everyone has the right to education. Education shall be free, at least in the elementary and fundamental stages. Elementary education shall be compulsory. Technical and professional education shall be made generally available and higher education shall be equally accessible to all on the basis of merit.

2. Education shall be directed to the full development of the human personality and to the strengthening of respect for human rights and fundamental freedoms. It shall promote understanding, tolerance and friendship among all nations, racial or religious groups, and shall further the activities of the United Nations for the maintenance of peace.

3. Parents have a prior right to choose the kind of education that shall be given to their children.

placed them in the context of human dignity. In adding this context of human dignity to that of the natural law definition of inalienable rights, UDHR broadens the scope of human rights to extend to issues such as workers' rights (Article 24), health and maternity rights (Article 25), education rights (Article 26), and rights to benefit from scientific progress (Article 27). In many ways, these articles reveal the tensions between Western liberal democracies that favored, at least theoretically, notions of political and civil rights, and the Eastern bloc led by the Soviet Union, which favored economic, social and cultural rights.

Several direct connections can be made between UDHR's Article 26 and UNESCO maneuvers in education. By the time the UN's Commission on Human Rights framed UDHR, UNESCO was well on its way towards implementing its programs in "fundamental education" launched in 1946. This program dealt broadly with overcoming forces of oppression and ignorance. UDHR would provide further impetus for these efforts. Among the often named stalwarts of the Human Rights

Commission—Eleanor Roosevelt of the United States, René Cassin of France, John Humphrey of Canada—Cassin had been closely involved with UNESCO as a permanent member of the Conference of Allied Ministers of Education and as a forceful advocate of the right of education itself. Cassin won the Nobel Prize for Peace in 1968 at the age of 89.

The second universal instrument that has shaped UNESCO's program in education is the 1966 International Covenant on Economic, Social and Cultural Rights (ICESCR). The Soviet Union, the communist countries, and most post-colonial countries endorsed this convention. UNESCO by this time began to focus on social, cultural and economic discriminations that stood in the way of universal education. ICESCR in general and its Article 13, in particular, were frequently invoked (Box 2.2). The ICESCR Preamble provided the broad context for the measures against social and cultural discrimination in education. It noted that "the ideal of free human beings enjoying freedom from fear and want can only be achieved if conditions are created whereby everyone may enjoy his economic, social and cultural rights, as well as his civil and political rights."

Western democracies opposed ICESCR for the same reason that they had been lukewarm toward UDHR. In neither case is it clear who would guarantee the rights, the issue known as the "justiciability" of rights. Eleanor Roosevelt herself emphasized that UDHR was to be understood as a general declaration of humanity's guiding principles

Box 2.2 International Covenant on Economic, Social and Cultural Rights

Article 13

1. The States Parties to the present Covenant recognize the right of everyone to education. They agree that education shall be directed to the full development of the human personality and the sense of its dignity, and shall strengthen the respect for human rights and fundamental freedoms. They further agree that education shall enable all persons to participate effectively in a free society, promote understanding, tolerance and friendship among all nations and all racial, ethnic or religious groups, and further the activities of the United Nations for the maintenance of peace.

2. The States Parties to the present Covenant recognize that, with a view to achieving the full realization of this right:

(a) Primary education shall be compulsory and available free to all;

(b) Secondary education in its different forms, including technical and vocational secondary education, shall be made generally available and accessible to all by every appropriate means, and in particular by the progressive introduction of free education;

(c) Higher education shall be made equally accessible to all, on the basis of capacity, by every appropriate means, and in particular by the progressive introduction of free education;

(d) Fundamental education shall be encouraged or intensified as far as possible for those persons who have not received or completed the whole period of their primary education;

(e) The development of a system of schools at all levels shall be actively pursued, an adequate fellowship system shall be established, and the material conditions of teaching staff shall be continuously improved.

3. The States Parties to the present Covenant undertake to have respect for the liberty of parents and, when applicable, legal guardians to choose for their children schools, other than those established by the public authorities, which conform to such minimum educational standards as may be laid down or approved by the State and to ensure the religious and moral education of their children in conformity with their own convictions.

4. No part of this article shall be construed so as to interfere with the liberty of individuals and bodies to establish and direct educational institutions, subject always to the observance of the principles set forth in paragraph I of this article and to the requirement that the education given in such institutions shall conform to such minimum standards as may be laid down by the State.

for the future rather than as a specific treaty.[4] Second, many of the provisions of ICESCR—in particular rights to form trade unions, and compulsory social welfare—were anathema to the idea of individual freedoms. For its part, the communist bloc pointed to the denial of equal civil and political rights from Western democracies to minorities within their borders and to the countries they colonized.

Despite these reservations, UNESCO proceeded to hearken both UDHR's and ICESCR's provision on education in its strategy and programs. Nevertheless, debates continue even to the present day on the specific justiciability of the right to education as well as other rights.[5] The issue of enforcement is unclear; are rights to education secondary rights in that they are important but perhaps not as important as life, liberty and the pursuit of happiness? Are they positive rights in that they are to be specifically provided rather than being inalienable? Finally, UNESCO has debated the notion of indivisibility of rights invoked to show that human dignity cannot be compartmentalized into specific types of provisions. In such a formulation education, health, and other forms of wellbeing are inextricably and indivisibly linked to the civil and political rights that ensure human dignity. The Dutch legal theorist Fan Coomans cites American economist and public intellectual J. K. Galbraith in debating the right to education: "Education not only makes democracy possible; it also makes it essential. Education not only brings into existence a population with an understanding of the public tasks; it also creates their demand to be heard."[6]

The education sector until Jomtien, 1990

The introduction to this chapter confirms that UNESCO became well aware, shortly after its inception, of the difficulty of educating humanity. Until the Jomtien conference in 1990, UNESCO had barely made any significant dents in educating, or in creating viable norms for educating, the world's illiterate. It struggled to define the contours of the education problem and to try to frame normative instruments for education, many of which reflected the global moves in enunciating the right to education.

Box 2.3 lists UNESCO's conventions, resolutions, and declarations in the field of education. While timelines are difficult to draw, early measures in the 1960s dealt with discrimination in education. From the mid-1960s to the late 1980s, UNESCO instruments focused on lifelong learning by addressing teacher shortages. UNESCO also designed instruments to recognize or compare education standards and diplomas cross-nationally. Since the 1990s, most of UNESCO's instruments have dealt with needs such as in technical and vocational education, and for training teachers.

This section describes UNESCO's first 45 years in education: the focus on fundamental education in the early years, measures against discrimination in education in the 1960s, and lifelong education measures since the 1970s. In significant ways, all phases can be taken to comprise

Box 2.3 Legal instruments at UNESCO for education, 1960–2010

- *Revised Recommendation concerning Technical and Vocational Education*
  2 November 2001
- *Recommendation concerning the Status of Higher-Education Teaching Personnel*
  11 November 1997
- *Convention on the Recognition of Qualifications concerning Higher Education in the European Region*
  Lisbon, 11 April 1997
- *Recommendation on the Recognition of Studies and Qualifications in Higher Education*
  13 November 1993
- *Convention on Technical and Vocational Education*
  Paris, 10 November 1989
- *Regional Convention on the Recognition of Studies, Diplomas and Degrees in Higher Education in Asia and the Pacific*
  Bangkok, 16 December 1983
- *Regional Convention on the Recognition of Studies, Certificates, Diplomas, Degrees and other Academic Qualifications in Higher Education in the African States*
  Arusha, 5 December 1981
- *Convention on the Recognition of Studies, Diplomas and Degrees concerning Higher Education in the States belonging to the Europe Region*
  Paris, 21 December 1979
- *International Charter of Physical Education and Sport*
  21 November 1978
- *Convention on the Recognition of Studies, Diplomas and Degrees in Higher Education in the Arab States*
  Paris, 22 December 1978
- *Recommendation on the Development of Adult Education*
  26 November 1976
- *Convention on the Recognition of Studies, Diplomas and Degrees in Higher Education in the Arab and European States Bordering on the Mediterranean*
  Nice, 17 December 1976

- *Recommendation concerning Education for International Understanding, Co-operation and Peace and Education relating to Human Rights and Fundamental Freedoms*
  19 November 1974
- *Regional Convention on the Recognition of Studies, Diplomas and Degrees in Higher Education in Latin America and the Caribbean*
  Mexico City, 19 July 1974
- *Recommendation concerning the Status of Teachers*
  5 October 1966
- *Protocol Instituting a Conciliation and Good Offices Commission to be Responsible for Seeking the Settlement of any Disputes Which May Arise Between States Parties to the Convention Against Discrimination in Education.*
  Paris, 10 December 1962
- *Convention Against Discrimination in Education*
  Paris, 14 December 1960
- *Recommendation Against Discrimination in Education*
  14 December 1960
  (Source: UNESCO (available at: http://portal.unesco.org/en/
  ev.php-URL_ID=13648&URL_DO=DO_TOPIC&
  URL_SECTION=-471.html))

an agenda for "Education for All" (EFA) that emerged in 1990. As early as 1946, UNESCO declared a program on "fundamental education" to educate the world's population. Presciently, education was conceived of as less to do with formal schooling but in terms of constructing humanity and its dignity through education. Librarian of Congress and poet Archibald Macleish, who redrafted Clement Attlee's "minds of men" statement for UNESCO's Preamble, described the broad and bold objectives of education in this radio broadcast in December 1945, one month after UNESCO's formation:

> Of course we can educate for world peace. I'd be willing to go a great deal farther than that, I'd be willing, for my own part, to say that there is no possible way of getting world peace except through education. Which means education of the peoples of the world. All you can do by arrangements between governments is to remove the causes of disagreement which may become, in time, causes of war.[7]

A poignant affirmation of UNESCO's education charter was the 1950 starting of UNESCO and United Nations Relief Works Agency (UNRWA) schools to educate Palestinian children in Jordan, Lebanon, Syria, and Gaza. War had devastated the prospects of education for these children and UNESCO stepped in. By 1971, an estimated 250,000 Palestinian children had been educated, a number now close to 1 million. After the 1967 Arab–Israeli war, Gaza schools were cut off but exams were set for them in Egypt and flown in through Cyprus. Later, with the help of the International Committee of the Red Cross, students were allowed to cross the Suez Canal and enter universities in Egypt. After Israel's bombings of Gaza in 2007, UNESCO similarly stepped in to denounce the bombings and closing of schools that affected the Palestinian children.[8]

Besides the success of measures such as the UNESCO/UNRWA schools, the overall "fundamental education" plan moved slowly. The program sought to work with people on things that would make their lives easier and by employing means that went far beyond formal schooling. The idea of the Sourcebook for Science (see Chapter 3) to teach science with everyday objects was, for example, born at this time. British humanist and peace activist Ritchie Calder, summarizing the first 10 years of fundamental education, noted in 1956 that the idea had gone far beyond highlighting the importance of education: "Men and women are taught how to till their fields better; how to care for the health of themselves and their children; how to look after their homes and so forth. In learning, they improve their conditions."[9] Yet, these measures did little to lift more than half the world's population, which was at the time illiterate, or half of the world's children, who had no access to schools.

Beginning in the 1960s, UNESCO shifted its focus to highlight the structural obstacles to accessing education and subsequently, in the 1970s, to promoting of ideas of lifelong learning. The 1960 UNESCO Convention against Discrimination in Education was an important measure. Article 1 of the convention defines discrimination as "any distinction, exclusion, limitation or preference which, being based on race, colour, sex, language, religion, political or other opinion, national or social origin, economic condition or birth, has the purpose or effect of nullifying or impairing equality of treatment in education."[10] Pedagogy in the 1960s, especially in post-colonial environments, was described in terms of oppression and subsequent consciousness awakening. Paulo Freire's thesis in *The Pedagogy of the Oppressed*, for example, reflected ideas about literacy being more than schooling and, importantly, showed that education that did not awaken human consciousness to oppression and discrimination was not liberating. Freire's pedagogy reflected similar ideas about psychological oppression circulating among thinkers such as Rabindranath Tagore, Frantz Fanon and Steve Biko.[11] To this day, Freire's ideas continue to echo in UNESCO circles. Irina Bokova, the newly elected director-general, noted in December 2009: "As we have learned from Paulo Freire, learning throughout life helps us to understand our world and to shape it—individually and collectively. In his words, 'Nobody is completely ignorant. Nobody knows everything. All of us lack knowledge of something. That is why we continue to learn.'"[12] In a tribute to Freire's ideas about consciousness-awakening, perhaps, the first 25 years establishing literacy in the world were summarized in a *UNESCO Courier* essay titled "The Mind Awakening" in 1971.[13] In general, UNESCO's ambitious eight-volume *General History of Africa* was meant to serve as a counterpoint to the histories of the world written from the viewpoint of powerful countries.

UNESCO's intellectual thoughts on education reflected the times. It convened special forums in the developing world to understand and plan literacy objectives. An important measure was the Conference of African States on the Development of Education, in Addis Ababa in May 1961, and its final report thereafter.[14] Thirty-five African countries, several European countries, UN agencies, and NGOs attended the conference. Background papers included those from economists such as Hans Singer and Arthur Lewis, ranging from the importance of education for economic development to calculating the absorptive capacities and finances of national educational systems. The conference helped African states assess their educational needs and set medium- and long-term goals. This idea of educational planning and setting priorities was precedent-setting, and similar regional conferences and reports followed the one in Addis Ababa. However, the implementation of these measures lagged except for few minor achievements. UNESCO created its International Institute for Educational Planning (IIEP) in 1963 to help countries overcome and plan against structural obstacles to education. In 1964, UNESCO launched the Experimental World Literacy Programme, which dealt with ideas of lifelong learning. The First World Literacy Day was celebrated in 1967. The 1960s also moved UNESCO from bold pronouncements about education and peace to giving thought to educational planning. The idea of planning, seemingly simple, was new and reflected UNESCO's acknowledgement that progress toward education would be slow. Nevertheless, various ideas were tried to get around these obstacles. In the six states of Yugoslavia radio was used for education, and in Ivory Coast, for example, UNESCO implemented a program of televised education to get around teacher shortages. Important planning documents from this period include *The World Educational Crisis: A*

Systems Analysis, by Philip H. Coombs, IIEP director at that time, and the 1972 Report *Learning to Be: The World of Education Today and Tomorrow*, produced by former French prime minster and education minister Edgard Fauré at the behest of Director-General René Maheu. UNESCO did begin to raise resources from other specialized agencies in the 1960s. UNDP funds helped UNESCO train 40,000 primary teachers between 1961 and 1970. By the late 1960s, other UN agencies joined UNESCO, prominent among which were the World Bank, which in the 1970s began to fund UNESCO's educational programs, and UNICEF, which started primary education programs. Nevertheless, until the 1990 Jomtien conference, education programs were sidelined by UNESCO's geo-politics in the 1970s. The NWICO turmoil of the 1970s and 1980s affected adversely the implementation of educational goals. Budgetary shortfalls also followed the withdrawal of the United States in 1984 and United Kingdom in 1985, the regular budget for education declining from $106 million in 1980/81 to $68 million in 1990/91 (see Table 2.1).

Education for All, 1990–2000

The World Conference on Education convened in Jomtien, Thailand, from 5–9 March 1990, just when UNESCO faced a budgetary crunch and competition from other United Nations agencies over implementing education programs. UNESCO's official rhetoric, that Jomtien was a response to the growing threat to national budgets as a result of market liberalization, masked UNESCO's internal fears about losing its status as lead agency for education. The United States and United Kingdom, having pulled out of UNESCO, now backed the efforts of agencies such as the World Bank in education. The Jomtien conference was

Table 2.1 Biennial budgets for education: 1960–2010

	Total C/5	Extra-budgetary resources	Total
1960–1961	764,000	540,000	1,304,000
1970–1971	19,309,258	32,748,700	52,057,958
1980–1981	105,752,800	174,357,000	280,108,800
1990–1991	68,019,700	2,874,000	70,893,700
2000–2001	117,377,200	100,000,000	227,337,000
2010–2011	118,535,700	62,008,300	180,544,000

Source: UNESCO General Conference; Programmes and Budgets; and C/5 documents.

UNESCO's response and brought together 1,500 representatives from the organization's 155 member states and also from 125 non-governmental and 33 intergovernmental organizations.[15]
The World Declaration on Education for All emerged from Jomtien. The declaration's Preamble acknowledges UDHR's right to education but then poses the grim reality of literacy statistics:

> More than 40 years ago, the nations of the world, speaking through the Universal Declaration of Human Rights, asserted that "everyone has a right to education". Despite notable efforts by countries around the globe to ensure the right to education for all, the following realities persist:
>
> More than 100 million children, including at least 60 million girls, have no access to primary schooling;
>
> More than 960 million adults, two-thirds of whom are women, are illiterate, and functional illiteracy is a significant problem in all countries, industrialized and developing;
>
> More than one-third of the world's adults have no access to the printed knowledge, new skills and technologies that could improve the quality of their lives and help them shape, and adapt to, social and cultural change; and
>
> More than 100 million children and countless adults fail to complete basic education programmes; millions more satisfy the attendance requirements but do not acquire essential knowledge and skills.[16]

UNESCO's moves toward EFA helped to establish a seriousness of purpose. The convening of over 1,500 representatives provided impetus to serious thinking about education in the twenty-first century that the EFA declaration sought to implement. The declaration also authorized a Framework for Action to Meet Basic Learning Needs to meet the six goals that EFA adopted (see Box 2.4). Interestingly, the Jomtien World Conference on Education was not preceded by any other major convention or recommendation. This is in contrast to UNESCO's work in other sectors, or even in prior years, in education itself, when major shifts in strategy were always preceded or followed by UNESCO conventions, recommendations, and declarations.

The 1991 General Conference asked the director-general to convene a commission for deliberating education for the twenty-first century. In 1993, UNESCO established the Commission on Education for the Twenty-First Century chaired by Jacques Delors, which delivered its report *Learning: The Treasure Within* in 1996. In the inimitable UNESCO style,

Box 2.4 Six EFA goals: Jomtien (1990) and Dakar (2000)

1990 Jomtien conference	*2000 Dakar conference*
1. Expansion of early childhood care and development, especially for the poor.	1. Expanding and improving comprehensive early childhood care and education, especially for the most vulnerable and disadvantaged children.
2. Universal access to and completion of primary education by the year 2000.	2. Ensuring that by 2015 all children, particularly girls, children in difficult circumstances and those belonging to ethnic minorities, have access to and complete free and compulsory primary education of good quality.
3. Improvement in learning achievement based on an agreed-upon percentage of an age group attaining a defined level (e.g. 80% of 14-year-olds).	3. Ensuring that the learning needs of all young people and adults are met through equitable access to appropriate learning and life skills programs.
4. Reduction of the adult illiteracy rate to half its 1990 level by 2 000, with special emphasis on female literacy.	4. Achieving a 50% improvement in levels of adult literacy by 2015, especially for women, and equitable access to basic and continuing education for all adults.
5. Expansion of basic education and training for youth and adults.	5. Eliminating gender disparities in primary and secondary education by 2005, and achieving gender equality in education by 2015, with a focus on ensuring girls' full and equal access to and achievement in basic education of good quality.
6. Improved dissemination of the knowledge, skills and values required for better living and sustainable development.	6. Improving all aspects of the quality of education and ensuring excellence of all so that recognized and measurable learning outcomes are achieved by all, especially in literacy, numeracy and essential life skills.

Source: UNESCO (available at: www.unesco.org/courier/2000_03/uk/dossier/txt01.html; and www.unesco.org/education/efa/ed_for_all/dakfram_eng.shtml).

Learning: The Treasure Within is a philosophical treatise, almost a meditation on what it means to learn and be human. This is also not a surprise coming in the middle of Director-General Federico Mayor's tenure, favoring such intellectual and philosophical approaches. The report highlights several tensions that must be overcome through education: local versus global, universal versus individual, tradition versus modernity, long-term versus short-term action, competition versus opportunities for learning, expanding knowledge versus assimilating it, spiritual versus material aspects. While emphasizing all stages of learning from primary to lifelong learning, the report also spells out "Four Pillars of Education":

- Learning to live together—through recognizing others and discovering interdependencies.
- Learning to know—by combining broad-based and specific education
- Learning to do—through acquiring competencies that can be applied to a variety of tasks
- Learning to be—speaks best to the title of the report exhorting individuals to discover within themselves the treasure of reasoning, imagination, aesthetics, memory, communication, and physical ability. This pillar recalled Edgard Fauré's 1972 UNESCO report *Learning to Be: The World of Education Today and Tomorrow*.

For all its idealism and vision, *Learning: The Treasure Within* was not a practical document that spoke directly to the shortcomings in literacy detailed in the Jomtien declaration's Preamble or its six pillars of action. The 15-member Commission included several ministers of education and senior professors. The work of the Commission was divided into six areas establishing the relationship of education to culture, citizenship, social cohesion, work and employment, development and education, and research and science.

A decade later UNESCO called for another World Conference for Education in Dakar from 26–28 April 2000, but the consensus in the world of international education was that the Jomtien goals were far from being fulfilled. Several international NGOs, such as Oxfam and CARE, had pushed for educational reform after Jomtien but were disappointed. Kevin Watkins of Oxfam summarized the case well:

> We are worried that Dakar is going to turn into another talking shop where everyone reaffirms things already agreed, sets new targets and then, as after Jomtien, goes home, cuts the aid budget and allows debt problems to continue undermining education

systems of Third World countries. For these conferences to work, you need to create a public perception that there is a serious problem which people have to tackle. And you have to come up with solutions.[17]

Dakar 2000 to present

Jomtien prioritized education, Dakar institutionalized the goals. Education for All became not only a viable project for UNESCO and the UN but also for a number of other international and non-governmental organizations. It also received impetus in the Millennium Development Goals that the international community framed as the agenda for action in 2000.

Karen Mundy notes that until the EFA initiative, education was by and large viewed as a national priority.[18] Donors felt that education should be funded from national budgets and were especially hesitant to fund costs of textbooks and materials. When funding was provided for international education, it was tied to donors' political goals such as in funding scholars and in attracting international students. The global norm regarding the right to education was diffused, but there was a disconnect between international and national efforts. Chapter 3, in contrast, will show how moves toward science policy prioritization in UNESCO were reflected and mimicked at the national level. International efforts to boost the cause of education, such as through debates on the right to education, or via multilateral efforts such as funding from the World Bank, UNICEF, or UNESCO, must then be seen in the context of national education systems. The Jomtien conference was merely the first move to prioritize the issue at a global level, and while consistent with the right to education rhetoric, it was equally compatible with national agendas in education such as compulsory schooling and vocational training. The rollout of the Jomtien goals, however, was neither practical nor well supported with funding. Dakar would seek to reverse these trends.

The impetus to EFA in Dakar came from several factors, foremost being that sets of actor expectations and funding opportunities began to converge around this new international agenda for education.[19] International organizations such as the World Bank, UNDP, UNICEF, and OECD had continued to push the education agenda. They were joined in their efforts by strong coalitions of international non-governmental actors who believed in Education for All. The Global Campaign for Education, founded in 1999 before the Dakar conference, brought together not only national-level organizations but also such powerful actors as ActionAid, CARE, Global March, Oxfam, Save the Children Alliance, and World Vision International. The Global Campaign for Education also capitalized on the recent trends toward celebrity sponsorship and can boast of champions such as Shakira, Angelina Jolie, Nelson Mandela, and Queen Rania. They have been a considerable force in pushing for a global agenda on education.[20]

In September 2000, heads of state came together in New York to issue the United Nations Millennium Declaration, which included the eight Millennium Development Goals, one of which was education. The other seven are: an end to poverty and hunger, gender equality, child health, maternal health, HIV/AIDS prevention, environmental sustainability, and global partnerships. The gender equality goal also has an educational component. The MDGs build upon a decade of UN and other diplomacy efforts in rethinking development, and it is no coincidence that the education goals reflected the Dakar agenda. In fact, UNESCO became the lead UN agency designated for Goal 2, primary education, and the education part of gender equality (Goal 3A). Reflecting other moves in the international community, observers have argued that the MDGs represented "a global commitment and a framework of accountability."[21] Others have argued that MDGs also represented some back-pedaling from the Western world for having ignored development issues through the liberalizing 1980s and 1990s, when market reforms were pushed forward with greater zeal than social safety nets among multilateral agencies.

Whatever the rationale, the MDGs recognized new realities and partnerships. The eighth MDG on global partnerships is significant. It pushed forward UN Secretary-General Kofi Annan's Global Compact, which began to allow UN agencies to partner with businesses, NGOs, labor unions, and governmental organizations. Apart from designating lead agencies, like UNESCO for education, the UN system was also called in to set up monitoring and evaluation mechanisms. Table 2.2, for example, summarizes the World Bank's data monitoring of MDGs.[22] Similarly, the OECD set up the Development Cooperation Directorate to monitor the MDGs, through its Development Assistance Committee (DAC) that oversees partnerships with the developing world.[23] In March 2002, following meetings, the International Conference on Financing for Development produced the Monterrey Consensus toward monitoring, accountability, and the responsibility of recipient countries. In summary, these early maneuvers helped to absorb the EFA framework within a broader agenda for development and helped produce mechanisms that would move the agenda step-by-step and allow for evaluation.

Table 2.2 Millennium Development Goals in education

	Total primary enrollment		Ratio of female to male in primary enrollment		
	2000	2008	1990	2000	2008
East Asia and Pacific	93.5	94.4	94.4	98.7	98.7
Latin America and Caribbean	94.4	94.9	123.8 (sic)	96.9	96.7
Middle East and North Africa	85.4	91.7	81.8	95.1	96.1
South Asia	79.0	89.5	75.6	83.6	94.3
Sub-Saharan Africa	58.5	73.5	83.4	85.2	90.3
Low income countries	64.8	78.4	82.6	88.0	93.4
Middle income countries	88.1	91.1	88.7	92.6	95.6
High income countries	96.5	95.9	98.9	98.7	99.5

Source: The World Bank Group, Millennium Development Goals—Global Data Monitoring Information System (available at: http://ddp-ext.worldbank.org/ext/GMIS/gdmis.do?siteId=2&goalId=6&menuId=LNAV01GOAL2).

These factors not only boosted the EFA efforts in UNESCO but were also paralleled by many internal changes within the organization. First, Director-General Koïchiro Matsuura ushered in reform designed to make UNESCO a more streamlined and efficient organization (see Chapter 1). Second, the United Kingdom rejoined UNESCO in 1997 and following this move, the United States was expected to rejoin, which it did in 2003. At the very minimum, these countries' memberships would increase the budget for UNESCO (see Table 2.1). Education itself became the favored MDG among many prominent US actors. Former first lady Laura Bush, who started her career as a librarian, showed a personal interest in education and continues to be a goodwill ambassador for literacy for UNESCO. Then Senator Hillary Clinton joined the Global Campaign for Education as another celebrity ambassador, which ultimately helped UNESCO's own moves in education.

The Dakar summit led to six goals. Box 2.4 demonstrates that the Dakar goals both overlap and depart from the six Jomtien goals. Dakar's goals 5 and 6 in particular can be interpreted as being more realistic. Furthermore, as noted above, UNESCO became the lead agency for coordinating the education efforts for two MDGs. These were:

- *MDG 2*: Achieve universal primary education:
- *Target 2.A*: Ensure that, by 2015, children everywhere, boys and girls alike, will be able to complete a full course of primary schooling.
- *MDG 3*: Promote gender equality and empower women:
- *Target 3.1*: Eliminate gender disparity in primary and secondary education, preferably by 2005, and to all levels of education no later than 2015.

The progress toward meeting the MDGs and the six EFA goals set at Dakar has been slow. Table 2.2 shows that between 1990 and 2008, the ratio of female to male primary enrollment in low-income countries increased from 82.6 to 93.4 percent, while total primary enrollment in these countries increased from 64.8 to 78.4 percent. For the least developed countries, data are not even available, and data for total primary enrollment were not available for regional or income groups in 1990. At least from these figures it is unclear if the progress in MDGs was any greater in the 2000–2008 period than before it. Second, what percentages of increase were due to MDG prioritization versus national policy is also unclear. Box 2.5 delineates a similar mixed picture for the EFA goals in general. Reflecting mostly the global economic crisis, the biennial budget in 2010/11 is less than the budget in

Box 2.5 Some facts about EFA

Reaching the Education for All goals

There has been progress ...

- The number of children out of school has dropped by 33 million worldwide since 1999. South and West Asia more than halved the number of children out of school—a reduction of 21 million.
- Some countries have achieved extraordinary advances. Benin started out in 1999 with one of the world's lowest net enrolment ratios but may now be on track for universal primary education by 2015.
- The share of girls out of school has declined from 58 percent to 54 percent, and the gender gap in primary education is narrowing in many countries.
- Between 1985–94 and 2000–2007, the adult literacy rate increased by 10 percent, to its current level of 84 percent. The

number of adult female literates has increased at a faster pace than that of males.

... but much remains to be done:

- Malnutrition affects around 175 million young children each year and is a health and an education emergency.
- There were 72 million children out of school in 2007. Business as usual would leave 56 million children out of school in 2015.
- Around 54 percent of children out of school are girls. In sub-Saharan Africa, almost 12 million girls may never enroll. In Yemen, nearly 80 percent of girls out of school are unlikely ever to enroll, compared with 36 percent of boys.
- Literacy remains among the most neglected of all education goals, with about 759 million adults lacking literacy skills today. Two-thirds are women.
- Millions of children are leaving school without having acquired basic skills. In some countries in sub-Saharan Africa, young adults with five years of education had a 40 percent probability of being illiterate. In the Dominican Republic, Ecuador and Guatemala, fewer than half of grade 3 students had more than very basic reading skills.
- Some 1.9 million new teacher posts will be required to meet universal primary education by 2015.

(Source: Excerpt from UNESCO, *Education for all 2010: Global Monitoring Report—Reaching the Marginalized* [Paris: UNESCO Publishing, 2010], 4)

2001/01, especially with the decline in extra-budgetary support (see Table 2.1). Overall, UNESCO's latest Global Monitoring Report highlights the global financial crisis and the lack of funding as the most important factors stalling progress toward EFA.[24] It critiques a Fast Track Initiative set up in 2002 to funnel aid to EFA as being under-funded and inefficient. Similarly, the Global Campaign for Education has also pointed out recently that EFA faces a $12 billion annual shortfall and that the goals are unlikely to fulfilled by 2015.[25]

Furthermore, UNESCO officials note that neither the UNESCO secretariat nor field offices are well geared to achieve the EFA goals.[26] Accountability and field office coordination continue to present difficulties. Field officers must decide about their most effective approaches on the ground. Anecdotal evidence exists that contact with education ministries and heads of state can help establish broad educational priorities and financing for education. UNESCO officials cite recent initiatives in Brazil and Latvia. However, beyond this macro-level prioritization, it is hard to establish a plan of action with national commissions, NGOs, other UN agencies, and the educators themselves. For their part, the member states send unclear messages. Even member states which are quite sincere in implementing educational initiatives at home or are in need of technical assistance, take politicized positions in Paris when it comes to establishing strategic and budgetary priorities. In terms of monitoring, the Global Monitoring Reports and pressures from donor agencies on UNESCO are widely considered to be effective. However, in terms of financing, UNESCO officials note that most of their time is spent on getting the regular budget approved while it is extra-budgetary financing that is most effective in this sector in terms of program implementation.

Conclusion

In committing the organization to "full and equal opportunities for education for all," UNESCO's Preamble suggested a universal education agenda for the organization. However, the ambitiousness of such a goal may well have been beyond UNESCO's grasp and capacity. Karen Mundy notes that a "feature of the education-for-development regime was its profound decentralization and disorganization" from the beginning and that UNESCO never quite developed the political capacity to coordinate this regime.[27] Since 2000, UNESCO has been propelled into a leadership and coordinating position for a renewed EFA agenda, but it remains to be seen what it can deliver. Despite the importance given to the Education for All initiative, especially with the boost from the educational component of the Millennium Development Goals, one official notes: "over the last ten years, it's frankly all over the place."[28] While the MDGs are unlikely to be fulfilled, education is now definitely central to global development efforts. UNESCO seems to have also acknowledged internally that a broad and philosophical agenda on education is not easy to implement. While its efforts are now more directed, the philosophical legacy of reports such as *Learning: The Treasure Within* is hard to shake off in a staff used to viewing education through this lens rather than from the perspective of an international policy-making or development agency. Decentralization and the creation of field-office capacities and external monitoring mechanisms are effective moves in the right direction.

3 Making science

The letter "S," signifying science, was a November 1945 addition to the UNESCO acronym and constitution. The Cambridge scientist Joseph Needham is widely credited for pushing the cause of science during the CAME negotiations, especially in the three memoranda he sent to the scientific communities worldwide in 1944–45. The 1945 insertion of S in the organization's name is publicized in the organization's histories mostly in positive ways; scientific methods and outlook can be taken to presage progress and, therefore, the explicit inclusion of science in the organization's agenda links science to the cultures of peace and prosperity. On the other hand, its late insertion is also sometimes understood as a lack of prominence given to science. Science continues to be a poor cousin to other goals at UNESCO and the staffers in these sectors bemoan that science often gets left out at important General Conference and Executive Board meetings unless prominent delegates or officials push its cause.

The UNESCO Preamble and Constitution make it clear that education, science, and culture are to be fostered for the sake of peace. Article 1 of the Constitution is instructive: "The purpose of the Organization is to contribute to peace and security by promoting collaboration among the nations through education, science and culture. ..." However, it is unclear if links to peace and security through the program are to be direct or indirect. In a direct sense, scientists might be asked to participate in projects that lead to peaceful uses of basic science research or in projects that seek to enlighten people on the causes of racial prejudice. Indirectly, a focus on the environment might speak to the long-term sustainability of the planet. Nevertheless, this ambiguity in meaning can be problematic: in the indirect connections, the links to peace and prosperity may be unclear. In the direct approach, there may be some overreach in trying to foster peace through limited budgets and resources. Nevertheless, both directly and indirectly UNESCO envisions a positive role for science. Enlightenment and humanism inform the approach to science, especially in reaction to the Nazi era context where science had been enlisted for the purposes of fascism, militarism and ideas of racial purity.

In actuality science encompasses two sectors at UNESCO: one is natural sciences and the other is social and human sciences. As shown in Table 1.1, the natural, and social and human sciences respectively account for 19 percent and 8 percent of the regular sectoral outlays for the 2010/11 biennial. Interestingly, however, the two sub-sectors also account for nearly half of the extra-budgetary outlays for the sectors. Historically, the outlays for the two sectors have hovered around the 25 percent mark.

The following sections analyze the work of the two sub-sectors—natural sciences, and social and human sciences (SHS)—collectively. Unlike the other sectors in UNESCO, it is hard to find a single narrative or a major debate that has dominated these sectors. The "story" about these sectors is thus generally a patchwork of initiatives—this may be their major critique as well. The chapter first details the normative ideals fostered by the sectors, followed by a discussion of the multi-actor networks involved in the sciences. Norms here refer to general prescriptions for action designed at UNESCO and not just legal instruments such as conventions or declarations: unlike other sectors in UNESCO there are very few legal instruments for these two sectors at UNESCO (see Box 3.1). The last section presents a few of the specific programs and projects that the sectors have undertaken.

Box 3.1 Legal instruments at UNESCO for sciences

Natural sciences

• *Recommendation on the Status of Scientific Researchers*
  20 November 1974
• *Convention on Wetlands of International Importance Especially as Waterfowl Habitat*
  Ramsar, 12 February 1971; Protocol: Paris, 3 December 1982

Social and human science

• *International Convention against Doping in Sport*
  Paris, 19 October 2005
• *Universal Declaration on Bioethics and Human Rights*

19 October 2005
- *International Declaration on Human Genetic Data*
  16 October 2003
- *Universal Declaration on the Human Genome and Human Rights*
  11 November 1997
- *Declaration on the Responsibilities of the Present Generations Towards Future Generations*
  12 November 1997
- *Declaration of Principles on Tolerance*
  16 November 1995
- *Revised Recommendation concerning International Competitions in Architecture and Town Planning*
  27 November 1978
- *Declaration on Race and Racial Prejudice*
  27 November 1978

(Source: UNESCO, available at: http://portal.unesco.org/en/ ev.php-URL_ID=13653&URL_DO=DO_TOPIC&URL_ SECTION=-471.html; and http://portal.unesco.org/en/ev.php- URL_ID=13652&URL_DO=DO_TOPIC& URL_SECTION=-471.html)

Policy influences and education

UNESCO at its best articulates important proposals for peace through its networks, utilizing normative instruments, knowledge building, education, and information measures. At this broad level, UNESCO's influence in science can be seen in the decisions on science policy made at the national level and the dissemination of scientific education at the grassroots. While the limited budget and resources of the natural and human sciences sectors are too meager to affect the wide scope of activities that fall within natural and human sciences, UNESCO has been uncharacteristically successful at the level of policy influences and education. It is in its specific international science programs, as discussed later, that UNESCO often lacks prioritization and, at times, effectiveness.

UNESCO is the only organization in the United Nations with a unique mandate for science as a whole, though it is overlapped in this mandate on specific issues by other international organizations. Its scope excludes nuclear issues at the UN Security Council. But it includes issues that are part of the focus of the United Nations Environment Programme, the

International Telecommunications Union, or the World Intellectual Property Organization. This can be problematic for making policy in specific issues that overlap with others. Nevertheless, UNESCO has been at the forefront in outlining the importance of science programs generally in national policies and education.

The post-war thinking on harnessing science for humanistic notions of progress was reflected in UNESCO's push to encourage these endeavors through raising the cause of science at the national level. Martha Finnemore makes a compelling case for the factors that spurred UNESCO's cause leading to norm formation facilitated by an international organization rather than at the behest of member states or their demands. She argues that UNESCO "'taught' states the value and utility of science policy organizations."[1] While the United States, the United Kingdom, or Germany might have created science policy organizations for security reasons prior to the great wars, over 100 states in the post-war era responded to suasion from UNESCO. In the case of small or resource-poor post-colonial states, there was little or no demand for science policy organizations prior to UNESCO suasion. In the mid-1950s, Finnemore shows that transnational scientific networks like the International Council of Scientific Unions (ICSU) gave way to a shift in the postwar climate from "Kantian transnationalism to cold war Hobbesian nationalism" among member states in UNESCO. UNESCO meanwhile set up several science programs, like the interdisciplinary arid zones program, and established field offices around the world. While it remained involved in UNESCO's program, science policy was now refracted through state instruments: "States were now understood to be primary purveyors of development and progress. Thus, it was states, not scientists, who could best bring the fruits of science and technology to their citizens."[2] UNESCO officials would travel to various countries providing science policy advice, and in a few cases even helped to draft the legislation that would lead to the creation of science policy organizations in these countries.

Interestingly, although UNESCO documents acknowledge the role that UNESCO played in science policy deliberations, they seldom refer to it as one of the key achievements of the organization. This is in marked contrast to the way UNESCO takes credit for various achievements in other scientific areas such as environment, sustainability, and water issues. There may be some "UN speak" here in not overplaying the role of an international organization in setting up science policy agencies in member states, which may like to take the credit themselves for these efforts. In a 700-page anthology summarizing 60 years of natural sciences at UNESCO, there is only one short chapter on this subject.[3] Nevertheless, the chapter acknowledges the impetus provided by the UN to examine science policy issues and the explicit role of the Research Organization in the natural sciences sector, whose position was boosted, as it became the Science Policy Unit in 1963, and finally the Science Policy Division in 1965. However, there is also another chapter in this anthology that documents the decline of science policy advice in the 1980s, with some resurrection of the theme in the twenty-first century. Science policy had been modeled along the lines of Soviet planning or mixed-economy experiences such as France. Apparently this remained problematic for scientists who wanted science to be neutral and for a few member states such as the United Kingdom and the United States who eventually withdrew from UNESCO. "Some Member States, in the name of laissez-faire—and endowed with strong scientific potential, mainly in the private sector—systematically attacked UNESCO's science and technology policy program during each General Conference in the 1970s and 1980s."[4]

While science policy organizations proliferated at the national level, UNESCO began early on to focus on grassroots education in science. The links with peace were quite direct: Nazi science, including attempts to advance ideas of racial purity through pseudo-scientific means; and the dropping of nuclear bombs in Hiroshima and Nagasaki, had given science a bad name. Organizations such as UNESCO were entrusted with setting an altogether new agenda. In promoting the purpose of science among teachers and children, UNESCO was refreshingly direct and post-modern in acknowledging that science is not neutral. The *UNESCO Courier* wrote in 1963: "There is a fallacious idea that science is objective while the humanistic studies are subjective. This is complete nonsense. Science is always the record of someone's personal experience."[5] Such frank assessments would allow the organization to both repurpose scientific education while bringing into focus crucial issues of scientific ethics and human rights. This agenda was carried over into social and human sciences to generate empirical studies that illuminate prejudice, for example, in a project that brought together anthropologists and biologists to examine racism.

Science education was pursued through teacher training, science manuals, and setting up of prototype or model schools that UNESCO often financed. It also produced manuals and textbooks. The *UNESCO Sourcebook for Science Teaching*, initially published in 1956, remains a bestseller with over a million copies in more than 30 languages sold, and has been revised in over 25 editions.[6] The book not only spells out scientific principles but also makes a compelling case for the importance of science education. It shows science teachers in elementary and lower secondary schools how to set up simple activities with limited resources to introduce students to science through experiential learning. The *Sourcebook* was conceived around the time of UNESCO's creation and also points to the effectiveness of many UNESCO projects at that time with limited budgets. There were also ambitious projects such as the *Scientific and Cultural History of Mankind* project launched at the General Conference in Mexico City in 1947. Julian Huxley and Joseph Needham personally pushed the project forward and it was housed in the natural sciences sector, though later it was moved to the cultural sector.

More recently, UNESCO has begun a flagship program in 2005 to advance capacities for basic science policy and to further science education. The International Basic Science Program (IBSP) is one of the five major International Science Programs (ISPs) at UNESCO and cooperates with various non-governmental networks in its activities. Officials tend to speak of basic science programs in UNESCO as providing the organization with a unique competency.

In the social and human sciences (SHS) sector, UNESCO has fostered norms that have an empirical basis but also guide countries toward ethical conduct and respect for human rights. However, it is hard to gauge the influence of these norms at the national level. Unlike science policy organizations set up with the natural sciences sector's help, there are not any significant institutions at the national level that have resulted from the SHS sector's norms. In the human rights arena, adoption among member states, even of the 1945 Universal Declaration of Human Rights, is weak. UNESCO has also leaned toward the notion of cultural rights, which reflects the passage of the International Covenant on Economic, Social and Cultural Rights (ICESCR) at the UN General Assembly on 16 December 1966.

UNESCO has tried to follow its historic precedents and mandate in human rights issues. During CAME negotiations, for example, the need arose to empirically invalidate ideas of racial superiority. Its documents suggested, "How elementary anthropological and linguistic facts might be introduced into the curricula of schools and universities."[7] Especially in the 1950s and 1960s, UNESCO made important contributions to advancing the scientific basis of human rights and offered its expertise in notable struggles such as those against the apartheid regime in South Africa. However, the SHS sector may have been marginalized during DG Maheu's tenure, followed by the politicization and ideological pressures on the sector during DG M'Bow's tenure.[8]

UNESCO's social and human sciences sector has also been deeply engaged since the 1990s in deliberating the ethics of science and technology. Nevertheless, it has produced mostly declarations, not conventions, which possess a relatively weak legal status. Unlike other sectors at UNESCO, there is only one convention associated with SHS, against doping in sport, perhaps because of the practical difficulty of getting the states to agree on issues of human rights and ethics that are the purview of this sector, especially given the politicization legacy of the 1970s and the 1980s. Critics also argue that the term "ethics" is not defined and that different states have different notions of human rights. Nevertheless, the following chronology of normative instruments and deliberative bodies that UNESCO has founded in SHS does show that UNESCO has tried, at least, to tackle complex issues:

- Universal Declaration on the Human Genome and Human Rights, adopted by the General Conference on 11 November 1997;
- The 18-member World Commission on the Ethics of Scientific Knowledge and Technology (COMEST) came into being in 1998 and advises UNESCO on ethics issues in freshwater, outer space, energy, sustainable development, and information technologies;
- International Declaration on Human Genetic Data, adopted by the General Conference on 16 October 2003;
- International Bioethics Committee created in 2003; and
- Universal Declaration on Bioethics and Human Rights, adopted by the General Conference on 19 October 2005.

Furthermore, there are many within UNESCO who believe that private authorities, market systems, and commercialization dilute UNESCO's ethical agenda. One UNESCO bureaucrat notes:

> One wonders if an intergovernmental organization whose decision process is founded in consensus among more than 190 Member States—representing many cultures—can define and adopt clear, normative texts that are demanding and constraining in fields whose economic stakes are considerable. The International Declaration on Human Genetic Data, adopted by UNESCO in 2003, distinguished itself by not uttering a word on the commercialization of such data.[9]

The bioethics and human rights issues being raised at UNESCO are, however, greater than commercialization concerns. As human genetic data get coded, analyzed, and categorized, they raise concerns about species and eugenics. During the Nazi era spurious racial classifications were part of Nazi science and the subsequent genocide. The possibility of genetic data being linked to enterprises such as eugenics similarly raises uncomfortable questions about the alleged superiority of certain human beings. These are hard and complex issues for science anywhere: whether or not UNESCO is able to settle the questions on ethics, its lead in raising them to the global governance agenda is indisputable.

UNESCO networks

Both the creation and the diffusion of UNESCO's norms take place through its transnational networks, even if intergovernmental actors try to dominate the process. The inclusion of "S" in the organization's name came at the behest of several scientific organizations. Joseph Needham himself reached out to scientific communities in three memorandums, referenced above, and letters campaigning for a science sector in the CAME negotiations. At a broader level, the French proposal to model UNESCO along the lines of the International Institute of Intellectual Cooperation (IIIC), a non-governmental body, was reflected eventually in the explicit inclusion of INGOs and the formation of National Commissions in UNESCO's functioning. UNESCO itself has over the years created and funded dozens of transnational associations in various natural and social science disciplines.

The International Council of Science, renamed from International Council of Scientific Union in 1998 though it still preserves the acronym ICSU, was one of the first organizations to receive UNESCO support. It was founded in 1931 and by 1945, at the time of its association with UNESCO, ICSU had 39 scientific bodies and seven international scientific unions. It remains important to UNESCO's aims and purposes and goals. Most of the important programs launched at UNESCO—on water, geosciences, biosphere, environment, and others—either were started or advanced through ICSU. It includes scientific bodies from 117 member states, such as the National Academy of Sciences in the United States, and 30 international scientific unions.[10]

Sixty Years of Science at UNESCO lists 34 organizations that UNESCO helped to get started.[11] The World Conservation Union (ICUN) started in 1948 when it was known as the International Union for the Protection of Nature and Natural Resources (IUPN). It is now the world's largest NGO involved in conservation activities. Interestingly, CERN, the European Organization for Nuclear Research, known for the world's largest particle physics accelerator, also had its origins in UNESCO in 1953. A similar enterprise, modeled on CERN and with a cooperative agreement with it, is SESAME (Synchrotron-light for

Experimental Science and Applications in the Middle East) set up in 2003 in Jordan, 30 kilometers from Amman at the Al-Balqa' Applied University in Allan. Synchrotron light, produced from electrons rotating in magnetic fields, has a wide variety of applications including archeology, environmental issues, medicine, and nanotechnology.[12]

In social and human sciences, the use of the scientific method, defined broadly, was the impetus for UNESCO to create or link with organizations that would investigate the causes of conflict through studies of nationalism, racism, and other types of work. These initially came to be known as "tension studies." Although the work of SHS was slower and more limited than other sectors, the sector helped to start associations in various social sciences, including comparative law and medicine, to name a few. The International Political Science Association was created with UNESCO's help. The *International Social Science Journal* was founded in 1949 at UNESCO and continues to publish in the six official UN languages.

Other specialized agencies of the UN and intergovernmental organizations also overlap with UNESCO's agenda. UN specialized agencies with projects in fields that UNESCO also considers to be its competencies include the following: the Food and Agriculture Organization (FAO), the International Atomic Energy Agency (IAEA), the World Meteorological Association (WMO), the International Maritime Organization (IMO), the United Nations Industrial Development Organization (UNIDO), and the World Health Organization (WHO). Most of UNESCO's projects overlapping with other agencies deal with environment and sustainability issues. In the field of information technologies and intellectual property, two other UN specialized agencies must be mentioned: the International Telecommunications Union (ITU), and the World Intellectual Property Organization (WIPO). A great deal of UNESCO's extra-budgetary resources since the 1960s has come from UN programs and funds including: the United Nations Conference on Trade and Development (UNCTAD), the United Nations Environmental Programme (UNEP), the United Nations Children's Fund (UNICEF), the United Nations Development Programme (UNDP), and the World Bank group. The Global Environmental Fund (GEF) supported by the World Bank, UNDP, and UNEP is among the largest funds available for environment. Furthermore, the United Nations has appointed, especially through its Economic and Social Council (ECOSOC), various commissions and committees to study scientific issues.

The existence of various networks that conduct work in science and technology issues is not entirely a blessing for UNESCO. First, its agenda was not just overlapped but was actually overtaken by other agencies. A case in point is the creation of the United Nations Environmental Programme in 1972 after the Stockholm UN Conference on the Environment. Until then UNESCO had taken the lead on environment and sustainability issues but after 1972, UNEP did so, especially in the 1980s and 1990s when the United States and United Kingdom left UNESCO. Similarly, although UNESCO tried to play a role in the World Summit on the Information Society (WSIS) deliberations over information rights and the digital divide since 2003, it was overshadowed by the International Telecommunications Union. Second, UNESCO itself has not always known how best to utilize its networks. An important report in 2007 commissioned by the UNESCO director-general on the activities of the two sectors pointed to the lack of utilization of UNESCO intergovernmental and non-governmental networks as a key finding.[13] For example, the report pointed out that even in one of UNESCO's key competencies, namely water issues, there are at least 20 other United Nations agencies involved. The report not only recommends intensifying partnerships but goes on to mention specific associations. The following paragraph is instructive:

> UNESCO needs to improve its outreach, through an innovative approach to partnerships with other organizations, both within and outside the United Nations, with the aim of increasing programme effectiveness, complementarity and efficiency. At the international level, these include the International Council for Science (ICSU), the Academy of Sciences for the Developing World (TWAS), the International Social Science Council (ISSC), the International Council for Philosophy and Humanistic Sciences (ICPHS) and the World Academy of Young Scientists (WAYS), among many others. At the regional level, these include the Islamic Educational, Scientific and Cultural Organization (ISESCO), the Arab League Educational, Cultural and Scientific Organization (ALECSO) and the Organization of American States (OAS).[14]

Science programs

UNESCO has numerous programs in the sciences. The broad scope underscores both the vitality of the two relevant sectors and ability of the organization to stretch its budget. UNESCO staffers, in speeches and documents, are quick to point out that the organization was the first, or the most prominent, to get involved in issues such as global interdisciplinary science projects, sustainability, and biosphere reserves. Nevertheless, this broad scope also dilutes focus and the organization is often critiqued for not working concertedly toward any one particular mission. The programs described in this section were only a few of the prominent projects that the sectors have undertaken.

The contributions of the social and human sciences sector to broad thinking on issues of human rights and bioethics were mentioned earlier. With a limited budget it is hard for this sector to make the kinds of contributions toward a positive peace that may be suggested by research in the social and human sciences. Officials admit that their input is often limited to advice for capacity-building at the national level.[15] Though not limited to this sector, and funded at one time mainly through the education sector, the interdisciplinary Culture of Peace program highlights the kinds of initiatives that social sciences can make toward peace. The program arose from two declarations: the May 1986 Seville and the June 1989 Yamoussoukro statements on violence. In 1994, UNESCO followed with the Culture of Peace program. According to its website "the Culture of Peace is a set of values, attitudes, modes of behaviour and ways of life that reject violence and prevent conflicts by tackling their root causes to solve problems through dialogue and negotiation among individuals, groups and nations."[16] The program was specifically conceived by the Princeton social psychologist David Adams, who suggested it to Director-General Federico Mayor. It also followed the UN's 1992 publication *Agenda for Peace.* Initially the program was launched in El Salvador. It included development, education, intercultural dialogue, and democratic participation as its instruments. After 1996, other conflict zones—Burundi, Cambodia, Rwanda, and Mozambique—were included. In 1999, the UN followed with the Declaration of the Culture of Peace.[17] Ostensibly, Culture of Peace furthers a positive agenda: after hostilities end in conflict zones; a positive agenda of peace must be undertaken that furthers development, dialogue, and participation. Nevertheless, while the program has undertaken a wide variety of projects in various continents, its specific contribution to producing a "culture of peace" in the areas where these projects are implemented is debatable.

The Management of Social Transformations (MOST) program, launched by the social and human sciences sector in 1994, despite its lofty title, only seeks to inform policy-makers and stakeholders of the relevant research in the social sciences for managing large-scale social transformations. Scientific humanism may be taken to inform the program's philosophy.[18] The "tensions studies" mentioned above, which UNESCO tried to undertake in the 1950s, were limited to national frontiers. The MOST program has a global governance focus. It acknowledges global complexity, featuring the interconnectedness of peoples

and territories and demanding global solutions. In fact, MOST literature does not shy away from calling the program the think-tank of the
world in speaking of global problems.[19] From 1994 to 2003, MOST
focused on broad topics of global governance, cultural and ethnic
diversity, and democratic participation. More recently, under Director-
General Matsuura the MOST program has focused on specific projects
and assessing ways of making a political impact with its research.
These projects have assessed poverty in Latin America and the Caribbean, regional integration policies in Africa, the role of the state in
developing social policies among the Arab states, human safety issues
in Asia, ageing societies issues in Europe, and sustainable development
issues in small island states.

In the natural sciences, the links to peace can especially be seen in
the historical emphasis given to natural resources and the environment
in its programs. In a front page article on UN programs in science, the
New York Times wrote the following on 19 June 1946: "The UN's
Secretariat is ready to marshal the world's scientists for peace as they
were for war."[20] An early program was the International Arid Zones
Programme conceived in the late 1940s and which ended 1962. Interdisciplinary in nature, it considered the problems of arid zones around
the world but also examined sources of renewable energy, which established the basis of other environmental initiatives that were to follow
from UNESCO, including those in hydrology, ecology, and geographic
mapping. Emphasis has been given to cartography since the inception
of UNESCO, and the Arid Zones Programme prepared detailed maps
of these zones dealing with climatology and resources.

UNESCO subsequently became associated with a variety of maps
projects, though the soil maps produced between 1961 and 1978 are the
best known. Victor Kovda, the director of natural sciences, and a soil
specialist, spearheaded the joint project with FAO to produce the soil
maps of the world at a scale of 1:5,000,000. Other projects included the
Geological Map of the World at a scale of 1:25,000,000.

Not coincidentally, the cartographic efforts overlapped not just the arid
zones initiative in the 1950s but also the planning that led to the success of 1957–58 International Geophysical Year (IGY). In the 1950s,
the UNESCO General Conference in Montevideo, Uruguay, passed a
resolution that led in 1955 to the creation of the International Advisory Committee on Marine Science (IACOMS), which could boast of
leading oceanographic scientists. IACOMS not only facilitated the
work of the IGY but would also bring together Western and Eastern
scientists during the Cold War, and showed that scientific cooperation
was possible despite political difficulties. The need for this scientific

cooperation was also felt after the Soviets launched the earth-orbiting satellite Sputnik in 1957.

Many of UNESCO's International Science Programmes (ISPs), as they are known at present, can be traced back to the 1960s and to the projects outlined above. These include the International Hydrology Programme (IHP), the International Geosciences Programme (IGSP), the Man and the Biosphere (MAB) Programme, the International Oceanographic Commission (IOC), and the International Basic Sciences Programme (IBSP, mentioned above). The IGSP, known as the International Geological Correlation Programme until 2003, is a joint initiative with the International Union of Geological Scientists (IUGS), and came into being in 1972. It researches the earth sciences and boasts of 400 projects dealing with earth's resources, including water, and with natural disasters. Specific projects range from studies of expansion and contraction of deserts to, more recently, those of climate change.[21]

In 1961, UNESCO began work on raising awareness of water resources, which received the support of International Association of Hydrological Sciences (IAHS). The International Hydrological Decade (1965–74) established the IHP National Committees that exist to the present day. Since the 1990s, IHP has become more closely connected with sustainability and ethics issues. COMEST has, for example, taken up these issues with IHP through the sub-committee on the Ethics of Fresh Water. The research and training wing, the UNESCO-IHE Institute for Water Education in Delft, Netherlands, was established in 1957. Apart from including hydrological and environmental sciences, the Institute also emphasizes economics, sociology, and management.

Cooperation with FAO, which began in 1955, led to the creation of the Intergovernmental Oceanographic Commission in 1960. IACOMS was involved in early planning. Specifically, a 1960 conference on oceanographic research in Copenhagen—organized in cooperation with other UN specialized agencies such as FAO, IAEA, and WMO—recommended the formation of IOC. The IOC is now considered a flagship program within UNESCO. From the mid-1960s onwards, the IOC also benefited from moves in the UN, especially the General Assembly, to further international cooperation in the oceans. In 1973, the General Assembly convened the third UN Conference on the Law of the Sea (UNCLOS) that led to negotiations on the use of ocean resources as a common heritage of humankind.[22] A treaty on the law of the sea was signed by 1982 and came into force in 1994, signed by 158 countries and the European Union. IOC's technical expertise was well recognized in the UNCLOS negotiations, especially for issues of marine pollution, scientific research, and technology transfer.

IOC has also produced a number of practical applications from its research and data activities. In 1965, it set up the Pacific Tsunami Warning System (PTWS). After the December 2004 Tsunami, IOC has been setting up the Indian Ocean Tsunami Warning System (IOTWS). IOC data and information are also important for the work of IGOSS (Integrated Global Ocean Stations System) for international exchange of data and information on the oceans. The IGOSS name was changed to Integrated Global Ocean Services System in the mid-1980s. In 1990, a working committee for ocean sea level measurements was set up called the Global Sea Level Observing System (GLOSS). The work of IGOSS and GLOSS in the 1990s led to the creation of the Global Ocean Observing System (GOOS), considered to be one of the premier information systems for oceanography. IOC's prominence within UNESCO has not come without challenges. The IOC budget receives special consideration in the biennial C/5 documents and stands alone from the budget of other ISPs. IOC's relationship with the natural sciences sector is that of a jewel in the crown, but it often resents any attempts at coordination from its parent.

Another major initiative, the Man and the Biosphere (MAB) program, was launched in 1970 to outline relations between human beings and sustainable development, the term biosphere itself referring to the layers around earth within which biological life is possible. It followed the Intergovernmental Conference of Experts on the Scientific Basis for Rational Use and Conservation of the Resources of the Biosphere, held in Paris in September 1968. At present, MAB is most commonly associated with the World Network of Biosphere Reserves to either maintain or restore ecological reserves close to their natural state. Biospheres are named after recommendations from national governments. The first biosphere reserve was selected in 1976 and the early biosphere reserves were mostly national parks requiring minimal restoration that were maintained by governments. Since then, biospheres have included reserves that needed efforts directed toward sustainable development and logistical support. As of January 2010, there were 553 sites in 107 countries, of which 47 are in the United States.

Biospheres include a core area with minimal human activity, a buffer zone where human activity must conform to the needs of the core zone, and a transition area with human settlements, including locals and others, working together in ways that are ecologically sustainable. The three main goals of biosphere reserves are ecosystems maintenance or biological conservation, sustainable development, and logistical support from international networks. A few of the biosphere reserves included are also World Natural Heritage sites. The natural sciences sector implements the natural sites included in the World Heritage Convention of 1972—this program will be discussed in Chapter 4. In March 1995, the MAB program received a boost from the International Conference on Biosphere Reserves in Seville, Spain. The Seville strategy for biosphere reserves was approved at the November 1995 General Conference.

Conclusion

The norms literature in international relations has celebrated the proliferation of science policy organizations as UNESCO socialized governments to the importance of science.[23] UNESCO has also been successful at local level with science education in schools using its *Sourcebook for Science* and other programs. The current International Science programs may be understood similarly as instances of intergovernmentalism, wherein sub-national organizations involved in science cooperate with one another. Anne-Marie Slaughter points out that such horizontal networks joining each other at sub-national levels are an important aspect of the new world order.[24] Given such a record in natural science with intergovernmental cooperation, it is ironic that governments have not cooperated, or been socialized, in UNESCO's endeavor from its social and human sciences sector. Perhaps, it is easier to cooperate in natural sciences, which may be viewed as neutral, while it is harder to do so for SHS with its highly complex and political issues such as human rights, bioethics, and social transformations.

Despite the efforts and achievements, an account of the programs for the two sectors seems like a vast mosaic of activities. Especially, the links to peace are hard to discern unless we view them at an abstract level of studying structural causes of violence and social unrest through phenomena such as technical changes, earth's tectonic shifts, or climate change. At this level, though, the question of relevance and scope become important. A scathing critique of UNESCO's science programs, quoting the 2007 report, also referred to above in the context of UNESCO's networks, summarizes their activities: "UNESCO has over time lost its leadership credibility as an international spokesman for science, and its programs are now seen by the scientific community as fragmented, over-ambitious, unfocused and lacking a clear vision and scientific strategy."[25]

The S in UNESCO endows the organization with a unique mandate, and this is often pointed out in the organization's literature and its assessments. However, it remains an isolated S. Even though the two science sectors are examined jointly here, they often do not cooperate.

This leaves open the question of intersectoral cooperation with education, culture, and communication and information. The lack of cooperation and focus cannot just be a result of lack of resources alone, which are not meager either compared to other sectors: the $185 million of extra-budgetary resources for natural sciences in the 2010/11 biennial is three times what education received (Table 1.1). For their part, UNESCO officials note that natural sciences are not well understood in UNESCO and that issues raised in social and human sciences, such as bioethics, are often hard for states to adopt. Often times, the sciences sectors depend on prioritization from UNESCO's Executive Board members who might themselves be scientists.[26] A better dialogue with other sectors and some clarification at the UN level of the roles of various science organizations may be needed to prioritize the sciences within UNESCO.

4 The prominence of culture

In most people's minds, the acronym UNESCO evokes something about culture. Many in the media also report only the cultural aspects of UNESCO. After the September 2009 election of Irina Bokova as director-general, the BBC referred to UNESCO as the cultural organization of the United Nations.[1] As people travel around the world, be it to the Machu Picchu sanctuary or the historic spiritual capital of Timbuktu in Mali, they are most likely to find references to UNESCO at World Heritage sites, a program initiated by UNESCO in 1972. As of March 2010, there were 890 World Heritage sites. By any estimate the World Heritage program through UNESCO is its most successful and widely known initiative. Culture, nevertheless, cannot be limited to world heritage and, second, notions of heritage themselves have been subject to scrutiny, both inside and outside of UNESCO. This chapter first attends to the heritage program before discussing the far greater program on maintaining and creating cultural diversity for the task of socio-economic development.

UNESCO's Preamble and Constitution provide the first instances of a broad definition of culture. If defenses of peace are to originate in the minds of human beings, then the organization is asking for cultural and transformational shifts in the ways in which we live and interact. Right after the "minds of men" statement, the Preamble continues thus:

> That ignorance of each other's ways and lives has been a common cause, throughout the history of mankind, of that suspicion and mistrust between the peoples of the world through which their differences have all too often broken into war;

And, one sentence later:

> That the wide diffusion of culture, and the education of humanity for justice and liberty and peace are indispensable to the dignity of

man and constitute a sacred duty which all the nations must fulfil
in a spirit of mutual assistance and concern.

Any discussion on heritage or cultural diversity must then be viewed
from the broad principles of the Preamble. It is to UNESCO's credit
that in cultural issues the connection to these principles is quite explicit, further accounting for this sector's salience. Laurent Lévi-Strauss
observes that UNESCO's World Heritage program has been moving
from a "monumentalist" vision to a more "anthropological" vision.
This is equally apt for UNESCO's work in culture, which continues to
shift away from a consideration of monuments and other cultural artifacts to considering culture as a way of life.[2] At it does so, UNESCO
also faces the danger of becoming too broad and ideal in objectives while
trying to balance that against the immediate needs and the politics that
inform the agenda-setting in an organization with limited funds and
capacity.

Cultural heritage

Culture can be taken to mean human beings' aesthetic, symbolic or
linguistic expressions, or it can encompass a community or organization's
ways of life. While related, the former refers to human creative endeavors, the latter to everyday life. Ideas of heritage conservation and preservation originated in the nineteenth century and were initially meant for
cultural expressions in the aesthetic sense, and until quite recently at
UNESCO, these ideas favored iconic cultural expressions such as the
Taj Mahal or the cathedral of Notre Dame. UNESCO continues its
preservation work but simultaneously works to broaden definitions of
heritage. The Convention on Intangible Cultural Heritage discussed
later is an important instrument of the broadening notion.

The idea of heritage conservation originates in the nineteenth century. Art critic and poet John Ruskin noted in 1880 that preserving
historical architecture was a necessity in the midst of the Industrial
Revolution: "*We have no right whatsoever to touch them. They are not
ours. They belong partly to those who built them, and partly to all
generations of mankind who are to follow.*"[3] While our current conceptions of universal value in world heritage may be traced to these
ideas, we can equally detect here traces of linear, imperial, and expert-
led thinking that would form the basis of critiques of these heritage
ideas. The British, for example, not only impressed these ideas upon
the world but also appropriated for themselves the mantle of curation.
They carried away, and continue to hold, treasures from around the

world in the name of conservation. The case of the marbles taken by
Lord Elgin from the Parthenon in Athens in the first decade of the
nineteenth century is perhaps the best-known example and continues to
cause strife. The recently opened New Acropolis Museum in Athens
features blank spaces in the exhibition area for these marbles to be placed
in when they are returned from Britain. Further afield in the colonies,
the British ideas of conservation removed agency from the people.
Cultural artifacts were preserved in various sites, while their designs,
photographs, replicas, and samples were taken to England: "Such
photographs of ruins and remote monuments are paradigmatic of the
'museumizing imagination,' a Western development that assigned the
colonized states a sense of 'tradition,' while protecting their cultural
heritage."[4]

UNESCO's ideas for heritage preservation are derived from these
nineteenth-century precepts. However, their concrete expression at the
global level first came from the 1913 international conference in
Berne to consider ideas of natural heritage of humankind. The subsequent
Brunnen conference in 1947 and the formation of the World Conservation Union (IUCN) in 1948 legitimated these ideas in the post-
war environment. Meanwhile, the Charters of Athens in 1931 and 1933
sought to preserve ancient monuments. These initiatives themselves
arose from the League of Nations International Institute of Intellectual
Cooperation, which served as a model for UNESCO itself (see Chapter 1).
World War II not only halted these efforts, but it also caused inestim-
able damage to monuments and architecture, and theft of art objects
that continues to make headlines. The Nuremburg Trials treated damage
to art as a matter of human rights.[5] A recent controversy pertains to
the actual or potential return of paintings by Gustav Klimt from col-
lections in Linz and Vienna to their Jewish owners from whom these
paintings were seized when they fled the Nazis.

The short historical preface above bears not only specifically upon
heritage conservation and preservation, but also upon the seven cultural conventions to come out of UNESCO (Box 4.1). Thus, in 1954
UNESCO adopted a convention protecting cultural property during
war, and in 1970 another convention that prohibits illicit transfers of
cultural property. The 1972 Convention on World Cultural and Natural Heritage is the best known, while the 2005 Convention on the
Protection and Promotion of the Diversity of Cultural Expressions
may be the most controversial (see next section).

The impetus for the 1972 World Heritage Convention, as it is
popularly known, developed out of campaigns to save the ancient
Egyptian sites at Nubia as the construction of the Aswan dam

> ### *Box 4.1* UNESCO's seven cultural conventions
>
> 1 Protection and Promotion of the Diversity of Cultural Expressions (2005)
> 2 Safeguarding of the Intangible Cultural Heritage (2003)
> 3 Protection of the Underwater Cultural Heritage (2001)
> 4 Protection of the World Cultural and Natural Heritage (1972)
> 5 Prohibiting and Preventing the Illicit Import, Export and Transfer of Cultural Property (1970)
> 6 Protection of Cultural Property in the Event of Armed Conflict (1954)
> 7 Universal Copyright Convention (1952, 1971).

proceeded on the Nile and threatened to submerge the monuments. UNESCO's Nubia campaign not only saved the monuments but also highlighted humanity's interest in historic preservation and, at abstract and poignant levels, the role of collective memory in human history. André Malraux's poetic siren helped to create a humanity around this cause:[6]

> But behold, ancient river, whose floods allowed astrologers to fix the most ancient date in history, men are coming now, from all parts of the world, who will carry these giants far away from your life-giving, destructive waters. Let the night fall, and you will reflect again the stars under which Isis accomplished her funeral rites, the star of Rameses. But the humblest worker come to rescue the statues of Isis and Rameses will tell you something you have always known but never heard from men before: that there is only one action over which indifferent stars are unchanging, murmurous rivers have no sway: it is the action of man who snatches something from death.

UNESCO Director-General Vittorino Veronese started the Nubian campaign in 1959, which moved in two phases, first for the monuments at Abu Simbel and then in Philae, and collected more than $40 million of the requisite $80 million from private and public sources internationally. Nubia is by far the most notable campaign that UNESCO has executed. It was followed by several international solicitations, including calls to restore monuments in Venice and Florence after the ravaging floods in 1966, the temple of Borobodur in Indonesia, and Carthage archeological sites in Tunisia. More than anything, these events created the momentum for the World Heritage Convention.

The 1972 UNESCO Convention on the Protection of World Cultural and Natural Heritage, signed by 186 states by 2009, came into effect in December 1975 after ratification from the requisite 40 signatories. The convention puts forward a framework for prioritizing, selecting, and governing a program of global heritage. A few features of the convention text are collected in Box 4.2. The introduction notes that selected sites need to be of "outstanding universal value." Article 8 specifies the governance framework. A 21-member World Heritage Committee is to be nominated from the states parties to the convention (Article 8.1). It is housed within the World Heritage Centre, which acts as the convention's secretariat. Interestingly, Article 8.3 is specific in outlining the advisory role for relevant NGOs, specifically the World Conservation Union (IUCN), International Council of Monuments (ICOMOS) and the International Centre for the Study of the Preservation and Restoration of Cultural Property (ICCROM). Article 11 details the process and criteria for drawing up the World Heritage List. A state party prepares the necessary application, which is then forwarded to IUCN or ICOMOS, which carries out the necessary on-site visits and evaluation. The 21-member World Heritage Committee takes these recommendations into consideration before inscription to the list.

The convention includes both cultural and natural heritage. As with cultural heritage, natural heritage has to be "of outstanding universal

Box 4.2 UNESCO Convention Concerning the Protection of the World Cultural and Natural Heritage

Adopted by the General Conference at its seventeenth session, Paris, 16 November 1972.

The General Conference of the United Nations Educational, Scientific and Cultural Organization meeting in Paris from 17 October to 21 November 1972, at its seventeenth session,

...

Considering that parts of the cultural or natural heritage are of outstanding interest and therefore need to be preserved as part of the world heritage of mankind as a whole,

Considering that, in view of the magnitude and gravity of the new dangers threatening them, it is incumbent on the international community as a whole to participate in the protection of the cultural and natural heritage of outstanding universal value, by the granting of collective assistance which, although not taking the place of action by the State concerned, will serve as an efficient complement thereto,

...

III Intergovernmental Committee for the Protection of the World Cultural and Natural Heritage

Article 8

1. An Intergovernmental Committee for the Protection of the Cultural and Natural Heritage of Outstanding Universal Value, called "the World Heritage Committee," is hereby established within the United Nations Educational, Scientific and Cultural Organization. It shall be composed of 15 States Parties to the Convention, elected by States Parties to the Convention meeting in general assembly during the ordinary session of the General Conference of the United Nations Educational, Scientific and Cultural Organization. The number of States members of the Committee shall be increased to 21 as from the date of the ordinary session of the General Conference following the entry into force of this Convention for at least 40 States.

2. Election of members of the Committee shall ensure an equitable representation of the different regions and cultures of the world.

3. A representative of the International Centre for the Study of the Preservation and Restoration of Cultural Property (Rome Centre), a representative of the International Council of Monuments and Sites (ICOMOS) and a representative of the International Union for Conservation of Nature and Natural Resources (IUCN), to whom may be added, at the request of States Parties to the Convention meeting in general assembly during the ordinary sessions of the General Conference of the United Nations Educational, Scientific and Cultural Organization, representatives of other intergovernmental or non-governmental organizations, with similar objectives, may attend the meetings of the Committee in an advisory capacity.

Article 11

1. Every State Party to this Convention shall, in so far as possible, submit to the World Heritage Committee an inventory of property forming part of the cultural and natural heritage, situated in its territory and suitable for inclusion in the list provided for in paragraph 2 of this Article. This inventory, which shall not be considered exhaustive, shall include documentation about the location of the property in question and its significance.

2. On the basis of the inventories submitted by States in accordance with paragraph 1, the Committee shall establish, keep up to date and publish, under the title of "World Heritage List," a list of properties forming part of the cultural heritage and natural heritage, as defined in Articles 1 and 2 of this Convention, which it considers as having outstanding universal value in terms of such criteria as it shall have established. An updated list shall be distributed at least every two years.

3. The inclusion of a property in the World Heritage List requires the consent of the State concerned. The inclusion of a property situated in a territory, sovereignty or jurisdiction over which is claimed by more than one State shall in no way prejudice the rights of the parties to the dispute.

4. The Committee shall establish, keep up to date and publish, whenever circumstances shall so require, under the title of "list of World Heritage in Danger," a list of the property appearing in the World Heritage List for the conservation of which major operations are necessary and for which assistance has been requested under this Convention. This list shall contain an estimate of the cost of such operations. The list may include only such property forming part of the cultural and natural heritage as is threatened by serious and specific dangers, such as the threat of disappearance caused by accelerated deterioration, large-scale public or private projects or rapid urban or tourist development projects; destruction caused by changes in the use or ownership of the land; major alterations due to unknown causes; abandonment for any reason whatsoever; the outbreak or the threat of an armed conflict; calamities and cataclysms; serious fires, earthquakes, landslides; volcanic eruptions; changes in water level, floods and tidal waves. The Committee may at any time, in case of urgent need, make a new entry in the List of World Heritage in Danger and publicize such entry immediately.

5. The Committee shall define the criteria on the basis of which a property belonging to the cultural or natural heritage may be included in either of the lists mentioned in paragraphs 2 and 4 of this article.

6. Before refusing a request for inclusion in one of the two lists mentioned in paragraphs 2 and 4 of this article, the Committee shall consult the State Party in whose territory the cultural or natural property in question is situated.

7. The Committee shall, with the agreement of the States concerned, co-ordinate and encourage the studies and research needed for the drawing up of the lists referred to in paragraphs 2 and 4 of this article.

value from the aesthetic or scientific point of view" (Article 2). Thus, the 186 sites on the natural heritage list include the Iguaçu national parks in Argentina and Brazil, Mount Kenya National Park, and the Great Barrier Reef on the northeast coast of Australia. The natural heritage list falls within the purview of the natural science sector of UNESCO and includes sites listed in the Man and the Biosphere Programme (MAB, see Chapter 3). A White House conference in 1965 had first raised the possibility of a World Heritage Trust on environmental issues but it was not until 1971–72 that the parallel movements for natural and cultural heritage were brought together into a single text after "a delicate negotiation."[7] The US position also reflected a domestic agenda: 1972 marked the centennial anniversary of national parks in the country. Figure 4.1 shows the World Heritage emblem designed by Michel Olyff. The square in the middle typifies humanity's creation enclosed within the circle of nature.

In the last 35 years, the World Heritage Convention has addressed several challenges, four of which are outlined here.

Organization and funding

As the World Heritage program grew both in terms of its lists and the parties to the convention, the need for an organizational secretariat outlined in Articles 14.1–2 grew immensely. The result was the World Heritage Centre, which began its work in June 1992 and brought together officials from both natural sciences and cultural secretariats. The secretariat coordinates the work of the lists and maintains contact with the key actors of the convention: the states parties, World Heritage Committee, and the INGO community.

Figure 4.1 The World Heritage emblem

Article 15 of the convention establishes a World Heritage Fund consisting of both obligatory (1 percent of each country's dues to UNESCO) and voluntary contributions. However, these resources are limited and total only about $4 million per year. States may from time to time contribute budgetary resources for specific activities by way of trust funds. Table 1.1 shows that in the biennial 2010/11 budget, nearly $16 million of the total $54 million regular budget is dedicated to cultural and natural heritage. While the budgetary breakdown for staff is not provided, if we take two-thirds of the budget as dedicated to staff, then it leaves less than $6 million for the program's activities.

Politics

All roads lead to politics at UNESCO. The World Heritage Convention was getting ratified by states in the shadow of the so-called Israel resolutions from 1968 to 1974 following the Arab–Israeli war in 1967. These resolutions called upon UNESCO to sanction Israel for damaging the heritage of the old city of Jerusalem either through its aggressive acts of war or through irresponsible excavations. Israel, for its part, protested that political rather than cultural considerations guided the work of these resolutions. The 1974 General Conference, in fact, condemned Israel for carrying out the excavations and, as noted in Chapter 1, Israel found itself expelled from its regional group. In October 1973, Raymond Lamaire was appointed a special representative of the UNESCO director-general for Jerusalem. While Professor Lamaire found no conclusive proof that Israel's archeological work was damaging the cultural property, Israel's indifference to UNESCO and to Arab and Christian sentiments was regularly noted by several UNESCO member states, including those outside the Arab world. Sagarika Dutt provides the following assessment:

> There (sic) was indeed no objective criteria for judging Israel's action and the position of each member state on the issue was determined by its own political, religious and cultural biases and predilections. Moreover, politically speaking, international opinion was so much against Israel, that there was bound to be very little sympathy for Israel's point of view in any controversy even if the issue was predominantly a cultural one.[8]

The Israel resolutions were the most politicized of all issues at UNESCO. The other politics of heritage at UNESCO are tame in comparison. In the 1980s the convention's politics centered on providing a balanced list so that a few countries did not dominate and there were efforts to limit the number of sites a country could propose. Second, the heritage list came under attack for being partial to cultural properties in developed states, especially those of the Western Hemisphere. Asia, Africa and Latin America would also argue that the way "outstanding universal value" was calculated seemed to privilege tangible and monumental cultural properties in the West, rather than the way these properties were endowed with cultural meaning. These critiques questioned core values of preservation and conservation as they had arisen in the West. Finally, states argued that natural and cultural properties were treated as binaries. In reality, cultural properties partly derive their value from the landscape in which they are situated, and natural landscapes frequently feature human tempering and enhancements, such as in the MAB program. These concerns led to an important 1992 conference in Le Petit Pierre, France, to consider these issues. In 1994, the World Heritage Committee accepted expert recommendations to make the list more representative, realizing that nearly 50 percent of the properties listed until then were within Europe. It also adopted the idea of listing "cultural landscapes" that featured both cultural and natural features.

Cultural values

Related to regional politics is the issue of values in conservation and preservation. First, the World Heritage Convention only lists properties of "outstanding universal value." Getting listed then becomes a badge of honor and prompts the international community and governments to prioritize the site. Economists have shown that countries featuring large inventories of heritage have low marginal value for specific items.[9] Singling out a few sites for the World Heritage List may further reduce the value of sites not listed while boosting the reputation of sites that are listed. However, the opposite is also true. There are positive externalities from these lists. As governments gear up their resources for heritage conservation of a few sites, they may now have capacity to attend to other sites. Tourists coming to hear musicians in Bamako, Mali, may think of a side-trip to Timbuktu.

A second issue of values is more serious and connected especially to the developing world's concerns on what gets listed. The prioritization of heritage is a subjective and, usually, an expert driven process. Who decides what these values should be and what do they mean for the communities who partake in these sites on a daily basis? Frequent complaints are heard in the developing world, that UNESCO heritage listing can amount to a cleansing process that alienates the local communities from these sites. Finally, heritage is an evolving concept. A cultural property may be seen as possessing little value when constructed but a few generations later, it might garner immense symbolic significance. This introduces other elements of subjective evaluation.

Sustainability and tourism

The idea of patrimony, to which most cultural heritage questions are related, is problematic. Patrimony etymologically means recalling the father, in this case the nation-state. The latter often constructs nationalistic or other meanings around heritage that instead of memorializing the past seek to create cultural understandings situated in the present.[10] Museums in China, therefore, present history from post-Revolution perspectives, Turkey downplays the Greek heritage of its monuments, and the Smithsonian in the United States generated protests in 1995 when it first displayed the B-29 bomber *Enola Gay*, which dropped the nuclear bomb over Hiroshima on 6 August 1945.

Questions of patrimony get even more complicated with respect to global factors, be they organizational pressures such as UNESCO's, or individual pressures such as those from tourists. Isabelle Brianso shows that the very processes of valorizing particular sites and the processes of UNESCO mediation may create tensions and troublesome meanings especially because the idea of heritage is a multi-disciplinary and evolving concept.[11] With respect to the Jemaâ el-Fna Square in the Medina of Marrakech, the square on the List of Intangible Heritage and the Medina on the World Heritage List, she asks if such listing takes away from the Square's "first vocation of producing conviviality and social bonding."[12] However, it is also important to acknowledge that its inscription on the list prevented its encroachment and destruction by developers.

Issues of sustainability have also come to the forefront with heritage sites in various other ways. First, the direct link between cultural heritage sites and domestic and global tourism has brought forth issues of environmental and economic sustainability. The United Nations World Tourism Organization notes that there were 922 million international tourists in 2008, a growth of 2 percent over the previous year despite the world economic slowdown.[13] Presumably, accounting for domestic tourists would boost these numbers even further. The top ten tourist arrivals, accounting for nearly 325 million international tourists, were in countries that feature a significant number of cultural properties, generating both economic resources but also considerable pressures on the environment. The MAB program as outlined earlier is concerned with preserving ecological balances. Tourist arrivals have been blamed for degradation in various natural and cultural heritage sites. Many countries now restrict the number of tourists that will visit their sites, especially if these sites are raising environmental concerns.

Another issue with sustainability concerns the List of World Heritage in Danger that Article 11.4 of the 1972 convention authorizes. This list brings global attention to those sites that are in danger of degradation due to natural calamities, wars, environmental factors and industrial developments, or tourism. Powerful examples of the list include the Old Mostar Bridge in Bosnia that was mostly destroyed in 1993 during the war between Bosnian Muslims and Croats. Since 1995, UNESCO mustered $13 million in support for rebuilding the bridge, which featured a confluence of Mediterranean, Ottoman, and Western European architectures.[14] The Mostar bridge re-opened in 2004 amidst great fanfare—the bridge symbolizing the co-existence of multiethnic society and peace as it had done in the sixteenth century when it was first constructed—and its re-opening was also hailed as a giant step forward toward moving beyond the horrific Balkan wars of the 1990s.

Until 1992, the List of World Heritage in Danger was drawn with the consent of states parties in question. Since 1992, the World Heritage Committee has placed properties on the List even without the request or consent of the state in question. While quite obviously a source of friction, the Committee's actions amount in practice to moral suasion and bring in reputational factors in order to induce compliance. Since

2007, UNESCO has moved toward further action by delisting sites, the first being Oman's Arabian Oryx Sanctuary that saw its Oryx populations dwindle due to poaching and oil exploration. In 2009, Dresden's Elbe Valley in Germany was delisted because of the construction of a bridge through the valley that, the World Heritage Committee in a 14–15 vote noted, degraded the value of the site.

Intangible Cultural Heritage (ICH)

The 2003 UNESCO Convention on the Safeguarding of Intangible Cultural Heritage came about in response to several factors. As noted above, the idea of tangible cultural heritage excluded vast parts of what peoples around the world considered their cultural heritage. The term "intangible cultural heritage" itself came from the English translation of the Japanese legislation on this issue dating back to 1950.[15] As defined in Article 6.2 of the convention text, ICH comprises "the practices, representations, expressions, knowledge, skills—as well as the instruments, objects, artifacts and cultural spaces associated therewith—that communities, groups and, in some cases, individuals recognize as part of their cultural heritage."[16] The ICH Convention also reveals the influence of UNESCO's movement toward giving importance to the values of preservation and conservation, themselves derived from ways of life or an anthropological definition of culture. Randall Mason and Marta de la Torre note: "A discussion of values connects the material and interpretive acts of conservation more closely to the social, cultural, economic and moral goals that drive these acts."[17]

The history of the ICH Convention can be traced back to the same period as that of the 1972 World Heritage Convention.[18] In the 1970s the Smithsonian and UNESCO organized various symposia on the issues of folklore and cultural life. Specifically, in 1972, Bolivia asked UNESCO to consider revising its Universal Copyright Convention to include folklore, and the 1980s General Conferences moved to request studies on protecting folklore. Initially, UNESCO and the World Intellectual Property Organization (WIPO) cooperated in their endeavors, but in 1985 UNESCO moved toward considering ICH issues beyond questions of intellectual property. In 1989, the General Conference with unanimous consent adopted the Recommendation on the Safeguarding of Traditional Culture and Folklore. This enabled UNESCO to create a program on Intangible Cultural Heritage in 1992, followed by the program on "Living Human Treasures" in 1993.

Several developments in the 1990s continued to reinforce the notion of ICH as it brought in parallel discussions of cultural rights (Chapter 2), international conferences on folklore and crafts at various international organizations (WIPO, UNCTAD, World Bank) and institutions such as the Smithsonian. In 1997, UNESCO, following the example of the World Cultural Heritage Convention, started a program to create lists of ICH through its "Proclamations of Masterpieces of the Oral and Intangible Heritage of Humanity." Biennial proclamations followed, listing 19 masterpieces in 2001, 28 masterpieces in 2003, and 43 in 2005. These proclamations included the cultural heritage within states, such as Vedic chants in India or shared across several states such as Maqam singing in the Middle East, Turkey, and Central Asia. By 1999, UNESCO formally began work on the drafting of a convention to address ICH. The election of the Japanese Koïchiro Matsuura as director-general in November 1999 coincided with and no doubt boosted these efforts. Matsuura had also served earlier as chair of the World Heritage Committee. He made ICH one of his priorities. Earlier, in 1993, the Japanese government had helped to establish in UNESCO a fund-in-trust for the safeguarding of ICH. The Japanese presence and clout is widely believed to have consolidated support for the ICH Convention, which was passed in 2003 unanimously. Inside observers note that the Japanese withheld support for the convention on cultural diversity (discussed in the next section) until the Europeans first supported the ICH Convention.[19] Initial ideas to roll ICH into the 1972 Convention on World Cultural Heritage were abandoned after considering the legal and organizational difficulties, but the ICH Convention is closely modeled after the 1972 convention in its provisions.

The ICH Convention may be taken to be a bottom-up initiative in many respects. First, as noted earlier, it came from similar initiatives in various countries. UNESCO's 2000 *World Cultural Report* notes that 57 countries already had cultural policies in place to encourage intangible cultural heritage and that 80 countries provided moral or economic support to creators and purveyors of ICH.[20] Second, Article 16 of the convention authorizes states parties to establish a "Representative List of the Intangible Cultural Heritage of Humanity." However, while the 1972 convention considers only properties of "outstanding universal value," the ICH List makes no such reference. Instead, as Box 4.3 shows, the initial nomination follows from community participation, which must be demonstrated to the ICH Secretariat and the ICH Committee, similar in its composition and rationale as the World Heritage Committee. While the ICH Committee makes the final judgment, it generally follows the community's criteria for adjudging the element to be of value. The first list was drawn up at the ICH

Box 4.3 Criteria for inscription on the Representative List of Intangible Cultural Heritage

In nomination files, the submitting States Parties will be requested to demonstrate that an element proposed for inscription on the Representative List satisfies all of the following criteria:

- R.1 The element constitutes intangible cultural heritage as defined in Article 2 of the Convention.
- R.2 Inscription of the element will contribute to ensuring visibility and awareness of the significance of the intangible cultural heritage and to encouraging dialogue, thus reflecting cultural diversity worldwide and testifying to human creativity.
- R.3 Safeguarding measures are elaborated that may protect and promote the element.
- R.4 The element has been nominated following the widest possible participation of the community, group or, if applicable, individuals concerned and with their free, prior and informed consent.
- R.5 The element is included in an inventory of the intangible cultural heritage present in the territory(ies) of the submitting State(s) Party(ies), as defined in Article 11 and Article 12.

(Source: UNESCO, "The Representative List of the Intangible Cultural Heritage of Humanity." Available at www.unesco. org/culture/ich/index.php?pg=00173)

Committee Meeting in November, 2009, in Abu Dhabi and included 90 masterpieces proclaimed earlier and 76 new elements such as the Argentinean tango and Indonesian batik. The notion of nominating and safeguarding the *process* that produces ICH, rather than the final product is especially important to the ICH Convention.

The ICH Convention has generated considerable excitement, especially in anthropological communities, but its critics note that the process is often driven by states rather than communities and that at its present funding levels, it suffers from similar capacity deficits as the 1972 World Heritage Convention.

Cultural diversity

The adoption of the 2005 Convention on the Protection and Promotion of the Diversity of Cultural Expressions showcases both UNESCO's efforts to make salient humanity's cultural diversity and the deliberate politicization of its own objectives by specific member states. The historical intensity and the lively political history leading to the cultural diversity convention are outlined below. The origins of the convention's ideas can be traced to the culture and development program as it grew at UNESCO in the 1980s and 1990s. Interestingly, the move toward this convention, which came in opposition to the liberalization of world trade in cultural products through the World Trade Organization, was a major factor pushing the United States to rejoin UNESCO in 2003. Cultural products, including films, television programs, and music comprise the biggest export from the United States. The rest of the world galvanized around cries of global cultural homogenization and Hollywood-ization, and began to support moves toward cultural diversity in UNESCO. The passage of the 2005 cultural diversity convention, as it is known, is by far the most politicized initiative to emerge from the first decade of the twenty-first century at UNESCO.

Our Creative Diversity

Historically, UNESCO with its World Heritage program had begun to explicitly promote the idea of cultural policies, but the links to development, in the form of alleviation of poverty and deprivation, had not been made. The 1982 World Conference on Cultural Policies, or Mondiacult, held in Mexico City tried to forge this link through an anthropological focus on culture. In 1987, Javier Peréz de Cuéllar responded to pressures from the Group of 77 (G-77) developing countries to declare 1988–97 as the Decade for Culture and Development. The idea of a World Commission on Culture and Development originated from this decade.

In 1993, UN secretary-general Boutros Boutros-Ghali and UNESCO Director-General Federico Mayor created the World Commission on Culture and Development. Javier Peréz de Cuéllar, the former secretary-general of the UN, was appointed its president. The Commission presented its report, *Our Creative Diversity*, to both the UN General Assembly and the UNESCO General Conference in 1995. The central lesson of the report is aptly summarized in the oft-quoted first sentence of the report's Executive Summary: "Development divorced from its human or cultural context is growth without a soul."[21]

The World Commission on Culture and Development was responding to various past historical and ideational developments in its report.[22] As these ideas progressed through the UN and UNESCO, they also reflected the link between culture and development explicitly addressed in colonialist and post-colonial literatures that questioned the oppressive imposition of "white" cultures in the colonial worlds. Writers such as Aimeé Césaire, Amilcar Cabral, Frantz Fanon, Leopold Senghor, Steve Biko, and Paulo Freire highlighted the oppression of the cultural factors of colonialism that assigned people an inferior status: only through a consciousness-awakening and a cultural voice from within would the developing world free itself of such oppression. "Poverty, national oppression, and cultural repression are one and the same," wrote Frantz Fanon.[23] In 1978, Edward Said's powerful treatise, *Orientalism*, recreated in meticulous details the genealogy of historical ideas in Europe that assigned inferiority to the Orient—its generalizability to all colonized and oppressed peoples was not hard to grasp among intellectual communities. Like Fanon and Freire, Said argued that the Occident created its superiority precisely by "othering" the Orient: "The Oriental is irrational, depraved (fallen), childlike, 'different'; thus the European is rational, virtuous, mature, 'normal.'"[24]

Our Creative Diversity reflects the dual impetus to bring culture into debates on economic development, while being starkly aware that culture must be understood in a liberating sense of an ethic that allows for diversity, pluralism, and freedom. The report argued that, "development embraces not only access to goods and services but also the opportunity to choose a full satisfying, valuable, and valued way of life."[25] It also took into account Samuel Huntington's provocative thesis on the Clash of Civilizations, which posited that the differences between the Judeo-Christian and Islamic-Confucian civilizations were irreconcilable and thus an endemic source of conflict.[26] *Our Creative Diversity*, instead, argued that cultural diversity should lead and not thwart endeavors of peaceful coexistence.

The report adopted UNDP's Human Development Reports, which, reflecting Amartya Sen's and Mahbub ul Haq's ideas, argued for development as entitlement to a dignified way of life. Interestingly, *Our Creative Diversity* report argued for competitive markets to assure provision of communication media services to people around the world. It also called for increasing the participation of women and young people, and public and private organizations at all levels of governance to mobilize people for culture and development. The 1998 Stockholm Intergovernmental Conference on Cultural Policies for Sustainable Development marked the end of the World Decade for Cultural

Development and followed the work of the World Commission on Culture and Development. The Stockholm conference sought to prioritize culture in development strategies and expand efforts to galvanize financial and human resources in support of such efforts.

A direct result of the *Our Creative Diversity* report was the publication of World Culture Reports from UNESCO in 1998 and 2000.[27] In an interesting twist, these reports started to feed into the momentum being created toward deliberating a normative instrument for cultural diversity in UNESCO. Prominent officials at UNESCO insist that *Our Creative Diversity* provided the original intellectual mandate and rationale for the 2005 convention on cultural diversity. Undoubtedly, the World Culture Reports take up ideas of cultural diversity and included officials and academics that would later lend support to the 2005 convention. However, the 2005 convention, despite its broad wording, was framed mostly to protect and promote cultural industries such as film and television and its chief supporters came from the developed world. The culture and development agenda that had developed in UNESCO was, in fact, marginalized in, and by, the 2005 convention. Recently, there have been several moves to bring culture and development issues back into the UNESCO fold but none of the three divisions in the cultural sector—heritage, creative industries, cultural dialogue (see Figure 1.2)—is specifically geared toward culture and development issues. Recently, UNESCO was named the lead agency for 12 out of the 18 projects that the Spanish government is funding for $900 million on culture and development. However, officials in UNESCO also point out that they are not a development agency. "In the field colleagues react as if we are a development organization. We are not."[28] Officials in Paris are more inclined to veer toward framing of normative instruments rather than participate in development project implementation.

Cultural diversity convention

Anthropologist Lourdes Arizpe, who supervised the efforts of the 1998 *World Culture Report*, writes that there are four groups of thinking in culture and development that are relevant: the first concerns those who question ideas of modernization and economic growth; the second concerns those cultural groups seeking inclusion; the third concerns cultural groups making claims that gain them political advantage; the fourth concerns groups seeking to protect their national markets in cultural goods and services.[29] The 2005 cultural diversity convention is centered on the fourth goal. A brief look at the threats to these national markets that developed out of the World

Trade Organization is necessary before delving into the politics that led to the convention.[30]

The politics analyzed here initially involved the United States and the European Community, in particular France, during the Uruguay Round (1986–94) of trade talks at the General Agreement of Tariffs and Trade (GATT), which later became the WTO in 1995. From the late 1940s onwards, Western Europe successfully argued that cultural industries, especially films, needed special protections such as quotas. During the Uruguay Round, the language of "cultural exception" supplemented that of quotas. This resulted in the European Union taking the now-famous most favored nation or MFN exemption, which allowed it to preserve its cultural industry policies.[31] MFN, unlike its name, bestows equal degrees of trade privileges for all nations: EU's MFN exemption at the Uruguay Round, therefore, allowed it the possibility of discriminating against US-based film or television products or preserving existing cultural policies that protected EU films or television against trade liberalization.

The main issue at the Uruguay Round concerned the European Commission's "Television Without Frontiers" directive that came into force in 1992 just as the Round headed to its end-game. The directive sought to reserve 51 percent of the total programs broadcast on any European channel to nationally generated programs. In reality, very few states implemented this quota but the EU position was to try to enshrine this quota formally through the evolving General Agreement on Trade in Services (GATS) at the Uruguay Round. Furthermore, inasmuch as US films and television programs dominate in Europe, the Motion Picture Association of America (MPAA) also argued that they were subsidizing European television and objected to the agreement sought by the Europeans at the Uruguay Round. Television programs in France, and in many other European states, are subsidized by film box office receipts, the majority of which are generated by American films. EU and US opposition to each other in these negotiations came to be called "la guerre des images"—"the war of the images"—in France. Transnational cultural industry coalitions among the Europeans led the way toward the MFN exemption that allowed the EU not to make any commitments toward liberalizing its audio-visual sectors. In the EU, this came to be known as the "cultural exception," underscoring the belief in countries such as France that cultural industries were non-negotiable.[32] France also argued that culture was also a national level issue in the EU and not among the EU competencies and, therefore, trade officials in Brussels could not make concessions in an industry that was not among their "competencies" or jurisdiction.

The decade following the Uruguay Round featured a progressive hardening of the European position on cultural industries, meaning that the EU would hold cultural industries to be non-negotiable, and resulted in the 2005 cultural diversity convention. Canada joined the Europeans in 1997 after losing a prominent dispute over magazines at the WTO to the United States. The dispute threatened to open Canadian markets not just to US magazines but also other cultural products. France and Canada joined hands in trying to develop an international norm on "cultural diversity," which sought national level protections for cultural industries. The norm strengthened their claims regarding the differential and special nature of cultural industries and linked these claims with cultural identity and diversity issues. Canada's culture minister Sheila Copps took the lead, in June 1998, toward establishing the International Network on Cultural Policy (INCP) in which France is a lead player. INCP brought together culture ministers from over 50 countries to exchange views on cultural policies. France along with Canada took the lead in getting UNESCO to adopt, on 2 November 2001, a Declaration on Cultural Diversity, which recognizes the specificity of cultural industries in particular countries.

The 2001 UNESCO Declaration on Cultural Diversity notes in the beginning that "culture is at the heart of contemporary debates about identity, social cohesion, and the development of the knowledge-based economy," and "that the process of globalization, facilitated by the rapid development of new information and communication technologies, though representing a challenge for cultural diversity, creates the conditions for renewed dialogue among cultures and civilizations."[33] It then defines 12 articles dealing with cultural diversity and links it to pluralism, human rights, creativity, and international solidarity rather than to the commercial considerations of cultural industries. Articles 8 and 9, listed under "Cultural Diversity and Creativity" are particularly significant in this regard:

> *Article 8—Cultural goods and services: commodities of a unique kind*: In the face of present-day economic and technological change, opening up vast prospects for creation and innovation, particular attention must be paid to the diversity of the supply of creative work, to due recognition to the rights of authors and artists and to the specificity of cultural goods and services which, as vectors of identity, values and meaning, must not be treated as mere commodities or consumer goods.
>
> *Article 9—Cultural policies as catalysts of creativity*: While ensuring the free circulation of ideas and works, cultural policies

must create conditions conducive to the production and dissemination of diversified cultural goods through cultural industries that have the means to assert themselves at the local and global level. It is for each State, with due regard to international obligations, to define its cultural policy and to implement it through the means it considers fit, whether by operational support or appropriate regulations.

The declaration came after considerable framing coordination among INCP and EU officials, shifting away from UNESCO's language. The frame used was "cultural diversity" rather than "cultural exception." On 26 October 1999, the Council of the European Union, in preparation for the Seattle WTO ministerial, declared that "the Community and the Member States maintain the possibility to preserve and develop their capacity to define and implement their cultural and audiovisual policies for the purpose of preserving cultural diversity." This was followed on 7 December 2000 by the Declaration on Cultural Diversity by the Council of Europe. The cultural ministers of the International Organization of the Francophonie adopted a similar declaration on 15 June 2001. An INCP working group on Cultural Diversity and Globalization met in Lucerne, Switzerland, on 24–26 September 2001, to finalize the plans for framing of such an instrument via UNESCO.

Along the way, the cultural diversity frame began to be linked to the biodiversity frame in an effort to provide international legal rationale to the logic of cultural diversity. INCP meetings were crucial in this regard. The INCP made an explicit connection to the 1992 convention on biological diversity framed in Rio de Janeiro. After the November 2001 declaration at UNESCO, moves were afoot to get to the next level of international law to convert the declaration into a convention on cultural diversity. At the World Summit on Sustainable Development in Johannesburg, Jacques Chirac, on 3 September 2002, speaking at the roundtable on "Biodiversity, Cultural Diversity and Ethics," noted: "One response which France proposes is for the international community to adopt a world convention on cultural diversity. This would be the counterpart to the Convention on Biological Diversity. It would lend the weight of international law to the principles couched in the declaration just adopted by UNESCO." He also noted that, "There is nothing more foreign to the human spirit than evolution towards a uniform civilization, just as there is nothing more hostile to the movement of life than a reduction in biodiversity."[34] At a UNESCO meeting in Istanbul, in November 2002, attended by representatives of 110 countries including 72 culture ministers, a declaration was adopted to support an International Convention on Cultural Diversity and to begin work on a draft.

The EU/French and the INCP then concentrated their efforts toward getting UNESCO to adopt a resolution to begin work on a Universal Convention on Cultural Diversity at the 32nd General Conference of UNESCO from 29 September to 17 October 2003. The United States rejoined UNESCO at the 32nd conference. This move is viewed alternatively as motivated by societal pressures within the United States, or as the US response to the processes underway for the crafting of a cultural diversity convention that threatened the country's biggest export industry, namely films and television programs.[35] Meanwhile, the INCP had already drafted such a convention, which was presented at its sixth annual ministerial meeting in late 2004. Apart from de-linking culture from commercial considerations and linking it with international human rights and biodiversity conventions, the draft convention courted developing countries by proposing a fund for capacity-building of cultural industries in such countries. In working toward a UNESCO convention, a number of other international organizations, academics, and think-tanks were courted by a network of INCP, EU and lobbying groups' officials. Developing countries, most of which have content and cultural industry protections in place, were viewed as key players. South Korea also emerged as an important example of a newly industrializing country that had rejuvenated its film industry in the 1990s with domestic incentives and protection mechanisms. The United Nations Conference on Trade and Development (UNCTAD), in cooperation with UNESCO, convened an expert meeting on audiovisual services on 27 September 2002, to help bring developing countries on board.

The INCP was also instrumental in creating a parallel non-governmental network of international cultural industry workers and artists that in September 2000 coalesced into the International Network for Cultural Diversity. Representatives, who would later form the INCD, were at the failed WTO Seattle ministerial in December 1999, in an effort to bring cultural issues to the meetings and also to organize protests against them. INCD, currently headquartered in the Canadian Conference for the Arts, is the leading arts advocacy group in Canada. INCD and INCP annual meetings and agendas run parallel to each other. INCD had drafted an International Convention on Cultural Diversity, which was similar to that of the INCP in its aims and philosophy except that it was more emphatic in keeping cultural industry negotiations out of the WTO. While Canada and France frame the INCD as a global network of non-governmental organizations, the imprint of the Canadian and French governments is not hard to discern.

The program for drafting a convention was presented at the 32nd General Conference of UNESCO in September-October 2003. UNESCO appointed a 15-member independent experts committee to further the issue. After several UNESCO meetings and drafting sessions, a preliminary draft was presented at UNESCO's third session of the Intergovernmental Meeting of the Experts, 25 May–4 June 2005. The draft was then presented at the 33rd General Conference in October 2005 and passed with 148 votes in favor and two negative votes, from the United States and Israel. It is known as the Convention on the Protection and Promotion of the Diversity of Cultural Expressions. The Preamble to the text starts by "affirming that cultural diversity is a defining characteristic of humanity."[36] Its 35 articles affirm the rights of nations to formulate cultural policies that promote cultural diversity and protect indigenous cultures. Article 20 establishes the relationship to other international treaties: "mutual supportiveness" is mentioned as the underlying principle but the convention cannot be subordinated to other treaties. In other words, if there were to be a conflict between trade liberalization and cultural protection mechanisms in the future, they would have to be resolved in the spirit of mutual supportiveness without subordinating the UNESCO convention. However, Article 20.2 then notes something that dilutes the precedence of the convention and may mean WTO instruments may supersede (if the EU was to make an audio-visual commitment): "Nothing in this Convention shall be interpreted as modifying rights and obligations of the Parties under any other treaties to which they are parties." Furthermore, as the convention's dispute settlement mechanism is not that strong, offering only a form of arbitration, the WTO dispute settlement process may still favor parties even against those that have not made a commitment regarding audio-visual product.

Meanwhile, US pressure did lead to the dilution of several other provisions in the draft convention, especially Article 20 on mutual supportiveness of international treaties and salience of obligations under other treaties. Nevertheless, the United States continues to assert that the very framing of the convention is not legitimate and that the convention is about trade and not culture. In one of the first instances where US officials addressed questions about the convention, a press briefing held by the State Department in April 2005, officials noted that because non-state actors initially drafted the convention, it was not legitimate. For an organization such as UNESCO, which has always interacted with non-governmental actors, this claim, even if true, is bogus and the United States also has a long history of working with non-state actors at UNESCO. On 3 June 2005, when the draft—which had then been amended and redrafted at an intergovernmental session—was presented at UNESCO and was being applauded, the US delegation—led by Robert Martin—staged a walkout and issued a press release which claimed that the convention was not about culture but trade: "Because it is about trade, this convention clearly exceeds the mandate of UNESCO." It goes on to note the following: "What we have done here in the past week has undermined the spirit of consensus that normally characterizes the work of UNESCO. It will surely weaken UNESCO's reputation as a responsible, thoughtful international organization." Soon after, on 30 June 2005, the United States, along with a select group of powerful states, presented a communication at the WTO's Council for Trade in Services. The select group included China, Hong Kong, Japan, Mexico and Taiwan—territories with significant cultural exports. Among other things, they noted:

> We express great concern over efforts by key participants in the negotiations to create an a priori exclusion for such an important sector ...
> We urge all Members to consider carefully the broad economic benefits from including audiovisual commitments in their efforts. Above all, trade in audiovisual services results in cultural exchange, the best way to promote cultural diversity.[37]

In the meantime, with ratification from the requisite number of states, the convention entered into force on 18 March 2007. There are several implications of this convention for the future global deliberations of cultural expressions. First, the convention stalls the global liberalization agenda on cultural trade while creating further momentum for an anthropological view of the value of cultural diversity. In the latter sense, the convention's agenda fits squarely into the broad processes at work in UNESCO. Second, and in opposition to the previous point, regardless of UNESCO's views on these matters, anthropologists remain divided on whether or not cultural diversity should be favored for its own sake. All cultures contain power hierarchies that marginalize the concerns of minorities and women. UNESCO must entrust governments to encourage cultural diversity within their borders, but often times governments themselves are the worst culprits in this respect. Ironically, a few days after the convention was presented to the UNESCO General Conference, riots broke out in several French cities, spearheaded by France's ethnic minorities, especially the Moroccans and Algerians, who find themselves excluded from political and economic processes in France. On 8 November 2005, President Jacques Chirac declared a state of emergency in France that lasted until 4 January 2006. Third, while the convention found broad support in the developing world, it effectively also ended the momentum built up toward making culture a part of development efforts through initiatives such as the World Commission on Culture and Development. The convention can thus be viewed as a Janus-faced instrument. While its context and preamble evoke broad notions of "cultural diversity," its specific provisions and implementation are geared toward regulating narrow conceptions of "cultural industries."

Conclusion

UNESCO's cultural programs have highlighted issues of collective memory, identity, diversity, preservation, protection, safeguarding, and the tangibility and intangibility of expressions. *Our Creative Diversity* is a carefully written document that acknowledges the dynamic, evolving, and polysemic elements of cultures. When UNESCO moves toward anthropological understandings of culture, it moves toward problematizing culture in all its complexity.

Despite their challenges, the UNESCO initiatives in World Heritage and Intangible Cultural Heritage symbolically embody efforts at preserving and safeguarding cultural identities and memories. The beauty of these programs literally lies in displaying and showcasing, through preparation of heritage lists and encouragement of tourism, the value of cultural heritage. At the same time, UNESCO is and will remain a political organization informed by the regional and ideological imperatives of states, which dominate its decision-making processes. It is unclear if UNESCO can succeed in encouraging cultural diversity through instruments aimed at specific cultural or creative industries. Human beings like their representations to be legitimated through images appearing on their film and television screens, and other creative expressions. UNESCO has been enormously successful in preserving relics of the past but it may not be as successful with expressions of the present.

UNESCO has tried to return to its roots in deliberating the dynamic aspects of culture and sustainable development its 2009 World Report titled *Investing in Cultural Diversity and Intercultural Dialogue*.[38] Director-General Matsuura's foreword acknowledges the work of the World Commission on Culture and Development and the World Decade for Cultural Development that culminated in the 1998 Stockholm conference. The report makes explicit connections to the Millennium Development Goals by highlighting the importance of cultural diversity in both proposing alternative visions of achieving these goals as well as the practical necessity in private and public organizations for making cultural diversity part of the organizational strategies and objectives. It remains to be seen if UNESCO will succeed in sustaining the momentum on both these maneuvers. As with its other reports, the 2009 report is eloquent on philosophic principles but laconic on practical measures.

5 Debating global communication orders

The most remarkable issue to arise in UNESCO in the twentieth century was the controversial debates on the role of communication in the post-war international system. UNESCO's forays continue into the present century with deliberations on the parameters of the information society and the digital divide. While the rise of democracy is intimately linked with the freedoms associated with the spread of information, never before had an organization debated the contours of this issue at the global level and tried to outline its implications for the very existence of the international system. The Soviet Union did not join UNESCO until 1954 because of the particular hue issues of media and journalism freedoms took with the push from the United States. The United States left the organization in 1984 partly because of communication debates at UNESCO, which were supported by the Soviet Union. Global orders must have ordering principles or patterns such as a hegemonic power, a balance of power, perpetual peace among nations, or international law.[1] UNESCO brought issues of communication into humanity's quest for a global order.

Communication in UNESCO debates has broadly and variously included the flows of messages and information, the content of the messages, the levels at which communication takes place from individuals to the global, the social and other stratifications through which it passes, and the infrastructures that enable its passage. UNESCO may have had limited success with the signing or enforcement of global treaties and conventions in communication but at an intangible level, its communication norms have resonated with both the thrusts of intellectual input and the expressed needs of societies and nations. Unfortunately, though, in shaping these communication norms, UNESCO itself has been deliberately politicized or it has taken a non-neutral position as a UN organization in aligning itself with political coalitions. It is important, therefore, to distinguish between the intellectual ideas and the politics underlying the communication norms that UNESCO has tried to foster. While there is a symbiotic relationship between ideas and politics, it is useful to keep them separate. Ideas can both shape and hinder politics or vice versa. In terms of the debates described below, for example, the ideational case for the role of communication in post-colonial societies was in large part made through UNESCO and related organizations, even if the politics at UNESCO prevented the case from being materialized into institutionalized norms. The ideas continue to resurface in other forms to the present day although the politics that enabled or hindered them have faded.

There have been three phases in UNESCO's debates on shaping communication norms. Earlier in UNESCO's history, the United States and United Kingdom pushed the organization to argue for press and media freedoms as the lynchpin of democracies and human rights. A second phase began in the late 1950s as post-colonial countries began to consider the role of communication modernization in their societies, which soon led to questioning the role of global media firms, mostly Western, in their territories. It culminated in the calls for a New World Information and Communication Order (NWICO) in 1978. The current phase has UNESCO playing a large role in disseminating ideas of the "knowledge society" that have been translated, to some extent, in the World Summit on the Information Society (WSIS).

The early debates

It is ironic that the United States exited UNESCO in 1984 partly over the communication debates. In an earlier period, the United States installed "freedom of information" on the UN's and UNESCO's agenda soon after they commenced their operations, even though the charter of the United Nations did not make any references to this subject. The US moves were motivated by three concerns: those regarding Nazi propaganda during the war; US fears and official processes underway to thwart communism domestically and abroad; and the country's history with First Amendment and press freedoms. At another level, the United States, the sole superpower after the war, came on to the world stage somewhat oblivious to its "city on the hill" image of dictating its ways to the world because it strongly believed it was morally correct and compelled to assert this position. The end result was a politicization of UNESCO and the refusal of the Soviet bloc to participate in its processes. In 1947, the issue led to the withdrawal of Poland and Czechoslovakia from UNESCO, and the USSR did not join it until 1954.

As outlined previously (in the Introduction and Chapter 1), in 1946 the UN General Assembly established a Sub-Commission on Freedom of Information and of the Press (SCFIP) as part of the UN Commission on Human Rights. The resolution also called for the UN to convene a Conference on Freedom of Information, which took place in Geneva in 1948 and was attended by 54 states.[2] Caroll Binder, a member of the American Society of Newspaper Editors (ASNE) and later also of SCFIP, noted that efforts to commit the UN to the concept of freedom of information "were successful beyond expectations."[3]

William Benton, US assistant secretary of state (1945–47), represented the country in the first two UNESCO general conferences and also led the efforts on freedom of information. He also presented the proposal for a $1–2 billion program, a phenomenal amount by any measure, for a worldwide radio network. In Congress, Benton called for a "Marshall Plan for Ideas" directed chiefly at the communist bloc. The United States was instrumental in passing through UNESCO two agreements for the circulation of information, especially audio-visual materials. These were: the 1948 Agreement for Facilitating the Circulation of Visual and Auditory Materials of an Educational, Scientific and Cultural Character (the Beirut Agreement), and the 1950 Agreement on Importation of Educational, Scientific and Cultural Materials (the Florence Agreement).

It was not hard for the United States to canvass support for its efforts because many of the UN's founding members were beholden to the United States in one form or another. The Eastern bloc at that time had only six members, of which the USSR did not join UNESCO, while Poland and Czechoslovakia withdrew. As the United States advanced its freedom of information agenda, the British and the French expressed some reservations but eventually went along. Among developing countries, Chile, India, Mexico, and Saudi Arabia were also hesitant. India was particularly vocal about Western media practices that distorted truth. Yugoslavia remained opposed. Despite this opposition, the United States was generally sympathetic for the developing countries' calls for technical assistance for building their domestic communication infrastructures.

The United States pushed hard on its freedom of information measures. While humanism as expressed through UNESCO instruments can be understood in terms of the spread of information and freedom of media, this was a contentious issue at CAME negotiations. The inclusion of this issue in UNESCO's Preamble was chiefly the result of US insistence. It was also generally believed that UN specialized agencies would remain non-political and technical while the UN itself would be the place to have political debates. Bringing these debates to UNESCO reflected both the inaccuracy of this thinking and the United States' ability to get its agenda on UNESCO's table.

It would also seem that the UNESCO Constitution's language of free exchange of ideas and contacts among people might facilitate the freedom of information that the United States wanted. However, this is not the way the rest of the world understood it. Julian Huxley was against information campaigns that were sectarian. Director-General Jaime Torres Bodet (1948–52) wanted to reduce the influence of the United States. Even within the United States, Eleanor Roosevelt and Archibald MacLeish wanted communication to facilitate global cooperation without causing tensions.[4] Many in UNESCO understood America's campaign as a war of words that followed the earlier war of arms.

When it left UNESCO in 1984, several progressive academics accused the United States of having politicized UNESCO for its own purposes in its early years just as it was accusing the Soviets and developing countries in the 1970s. While there is some truth to these claims, the timing and the level of intellectual exaggeration is troubling at both theoretical and policy levels. Theoretically, these critiques tend to paint US insistence on freedom of media and press as nothing more than a free market ideology of distorting information, pointing to media ownership and concentration in the United States. UNESCO itself sanctioned several studies correlating media ownership with lack of freedom. However, freedom of the press and media ownership are difficult to analyze and there is considerable debate in both scholarship and policy within the United States itself on these issues. To equate the effects of media ownership with free market ideology and non-independence of US media is debatable. At the policy level, to note that that the United States politicized UNESCO is understandable. But to note that every political process in the United States directed at UNESCO sanctioned such moves is an exaggeration. For example, Preston et al. confuse Assistant Secretary of State William Benton's stance with McCarthyism. No doubt Benton was zealous in his endeavors regarding freedom of information. However, during his short stint as US Senator, he introduced a resolution to expel Joseph McCarthy from the Senate in 1951.[5]

New World Information and Communication Order (NWICO)

NWICO represents the efforts by developing countries during the 1970s and the early 1980s to call attention to and to try to correct information flow and communication technology imbalances between the North and the South. While uniting the developing world with a common cause and producing heated confrontations with the developed Western world, these countries extracted few substantial concessions. The shadow of the Cold War and NWICO's support from the Soviet Union made the Western powers reluctant to give in to any demands. Major empirical findings at UNESCO documenting informational gaps between the North and the South got lost in the geopolitics in which great power security concerns rather than developing country demands dictated outcomes. The developing countries possessed few alternatives, and negotiation strategies also backfired. In the end, NWICO would be best remembered for its ideological confrontation. The next section delineates the scope and context of NWICO followed by the specific course that NWICO took in the 1970s and 1980s.

The context and scope of NWICO

The NWICO movement and negotiations are better understood as part of a growing developing world militancy and assertiveness in the post-colonial era. They also represent the developing world's acknowledgment of the importance of communications to the development aspirations of these regions. This runs counter to the current myth about sophisticated communication issues being unimportant to the developing world until the 1980s when these countries began to be socialized into the global liberal economy at a rapid pace.

As referenced above, developing countries began to highlight communication issues and point out the need for technical assistance from the early years of UNESCO's activity. In 1955, global communication issues between the North and the South were discussed at the Bandung conference where the Non-Aligned Movement (NAM) was founded. Of particular concern was the way the North portrayed the South in news media. In the 1960s, UNESCO held a number of conferences to help African and Asian news agencies counter these images.[6] By the 1970s, the developing countries were joined by the USSR at the UNESCO General Conference in denouncing the journalistic practices of the West.[7] The groundwork for NWICO was now laid.

The early history of these communication issues set in motion two processes, which would influence NWICO later on. First, the developing world's alliance with the USSR and radical academics was set in place. To the West, given the context of the Cold War, the developing world's concern with information imbalances was lost in the way the West perceived the UNESCO movement as a left-wing/communist-aligned initiative. Second, developing countries had in the post-colonial period placed an enormous amount of faith in state-led development efforts. Many of them drew upon the Soviet central planning models. The government was at the commanding heights of the economy in these countries. Communication issues thus also got linked with government control. Not only was the alliance with the Soviets quite natural here (given Soviet news agency Tass's acceptance of government control) but also it alienated Western media, which were built on the tradition of distancing themselves from the government. The Soviets presented the state as the embodiment and guardian of the people's interests and hence could not acknowledge any contradiction between state interests and media freedoms.

It must also be remembered here that the growing concern with information imbalances was an integral part of Third World confrontations with the North on a number of issues. In economic issues in general, the formation of the United Nations Conference on Trade and Development (UNCTAD) as a counter to the pro-market General Agreement on Tariffs and Trade (GATT) sought to provide more favorable terms of trade to the developing world.[8]

The idea that the collective efforts of the developing world to assert itself in global communication flows and representations would pay off was supported on numerous counts. First, there was intellectual support for the developing world cause in disciplines within and beyond communication and in forums beyond UNESCO. One of the intellectual founders of NWICO, Kaarle Nordenstreng, traced NWICO concerns back to the nationalist movement in the colonies and wrote of the four D's of NWICO: decolonization, democratization, demonopolization, and development.[9] At the broadest level, revolutionary intellectuals such as Frantz Fanon and Steve Biko pointed out that the mind of the oppressed and the colonized was enslaved through constant negative messages and stereotypical images. To Paulo Freire the liberation from oppression could only begin with dialogues, not the monologues or one-way flows of information that affixed the oppressed in a subservient position. Recalling Frantz Fanon, Biko wrote that "colonialism is never satisfied with having the native in its grip but, by some strange logic, it turns to his past and disfigures and distorts it."[10] Later Edward Said would follow in this tradition to point out the history of ideas in the West that would create the East in an inferior position through words and images: "the Oriental is *contained* and *represented* by dominating frameworks."[11]

Second, at a practical level, the experience with OPEC emboldened the developing world. It is no coincidence that the most vociferous confrontation between the North and the South came after the oil price hikes in 1973–74. Another source of support and direct link to the NWICO efforts was the developing world's demands for the New International Economic Order (NIEO) in the UN General Assembly. The UN General Assembly formally adopted the Declaration of Establishment of NIEO in 1974. It grew from the developing countries' perceived need to alter the terms of trade, which were seen as inimical to their interests (the so-called Prebisch-Singer thesis), which spilled over into other economic and related concerns. These objectives, many in the developing world argued, could be met only through better control over their own productive assets and the national and international norms which governed trading.[12]

The emerging importance of communications to the development efforts of the developing world might also be traced to two other factors: first, recognition of the importance of communications in general (including radio, TV, media) to the development process, and second, the explicit importance given to development of telecommunications in the call for correcting the communication/information imbalances between the North and the South. Developing countries had consciously adopted industrialization and modernization as goals for development. In fact, communication technologies were conceptualized as instruments to effect such goals for development purposes. David Lerner stated this categorically in the preface of an influential book on the subject. "Modernity is primarily a state of mind—expectation of progress, propensity of growth, readiness to change."[13] Scholars like Lerner effectively established the groundwork for the desired outcomes from mass media dissemination. Accelerating the following sequence could affect the march toward modernity:

increasing urbanization → high rates of literacy → mass media dissemination → political participation and economic growth.

These theorists argued that "modern" broadcast-oriented channels of mass media communication, as opposed to the traditional inter-personal ones, could help in replacing the "traditional" ways with much-needed secular mind-sets. In fact, as high levels of literacy are not necessary for understanding television and radio, these media were posited as being particularly effective for bringing awareness of political participation and social change.

The ideas about modernization and mass media would find full expression in Wilbur Schramm, who served as a UNESCO consultant, though later he was denounced by NWICO academics as a paid informant of the US government.[14] Schramm's seminal contribution remains *Mass Media and National Development: The Role of Information in Developing Countries* (1964). He held information flows to be essential to the development process, noting that mass media help the informational, political participation, and technical education tasks that are necessary for development. While radio does not require literacy and is as a result easy to deploy, print media, argued Schramm, are particularly effective precisely because they offer an alternative reality. The book was deemed quite influential in planning the mass media programs in the developing world during the 1960s and was widely cited in UNESCO's deliberations. Thus, communication development projects all over the world were used to provide distance education, and information on issues such as health, nutrition, weather, and farming. Information was often provided to affect particular goals; programs to induce child immunization, goading farmers to use better seeds or fertilizers, and to provide adult education fell under this rubric. While Schramm's ideas might have been initially limited to mass communication, they did highlight the importance of information to development. This led directly to examining the information imbalances within and beyond the developing world, especially between industrialized and developing countries. Later, this came to be known as the "communication gap."[15]

Two meetings in 1975–76 helped establish the framework for NWICO.[16] One was the December 1975 Intergovernmental Meeting of Experts in Paris, which continued work on what came to be known as UNESCO's Mass Media Declaration in 1978. It was prepared at the behest of the Eastern bloc and a few developing countries. The second was the 1976 Tunis Non-Aligned Symposium on Information organized by NAM, which brought together 200 representatives of 34 NAM countries. The idea of a NWICO was launched formally after the 1976 Colombo summit of the Non-Aligned countries and the 1976 Nairobi General Conference of UNESCO. The 19th UNESCO General Conference in 1976 at Nairobi, which called for NWICO, also appointed a 16-member international commission (known as the MacBride Commission) to investigate global media issues. The NWICO agenda was also endorsed by a resolution in the 31st UN General Assembly the same year. The same year, the NAM meeting in Colombo called for self-reliance in communications across developing countries.

Initially, the NWICO laid importance on correcting the one-way flow of negative news and information from the developing world to developed countries. But by the time of the MacBride Commission's report and its influential work, *Many Voices, One World* (1980), developing self-reliant communication infrastructures within the developing world became important. The MacBride Commission thus wrote that:

> Communication be no longer regarded merely as an incidental service and its development left to chance. Recognition of its potential warrants the formulation by all nations, and particularly developing countries, of comprehensive communication policies linked to overall social, cultural, economic and political goals. Such policies should be based upon inter-ministerial and inter-disciplinary consultations with broad public participation. The object must be to utilize the unique capacities of each form of communication, from interpersonal and traditional to the most modern, to make men and societies aware of their rights, harmonize unity and diversity, and foster the growth of individuals and communities within the wider frame of national development in an interdependent world.[17]

While seeking to correct the information imbalance (in terms of news and other information content flows) between the North and the South, what also emerged from NWICO were ideas emphasizing self-reliance in individual developing nations and collective reliance across them. Many authors and organizations during the 1970s, while not expressly endorsing NWICO, recognized the importance of self-reliance in communications and also emphasized making transfers of technology from developed countries more suitable to the developing world.[18] Before NWICO, Mowlana notes that the "[R]esearch emphasis on developing nations usually stressed how to communicate Western ideas and models *to* these countries, not how to communicate *with* them."[19]

Thus, by the time of the 1976 declaration for the NWICO, the stage was set for NWICO as an encompassing concept involving a number of issues regarding information imbalances. Beyond its philosophical and ideological aspects there was enough empirical evidence to show that these imbalances actually existed. In terms of specific issues, this would result in a number of sub-issue areas in which the developing world demanded parity, including information flows from the North to the South and the way that the North collected information in the South. As for the latter, the developing world felt that government controls were necessary. The main arena for these demands was UNESCO, while the process was also visible in the UN General Assembly, NAM and the numerous conferences organized in the United States, Asia and Latin America to support the NWICO debate. While the communist bloc supported the NWICO efforts (for obvious self-interested reasons), the West was quite opposed to it from the beginning.

The NWICO process

The NWICO process may be divided into two periods. The period 1976–81 witnessed rising militancy on the part of the developing world and the period after 1981 was marked by a harsh counter response from the West (especially US president Ronald Reagan and British prime minister Margaret Thatcher) which resulted in the United States and the United Kingdom pulling out of UNESCO. The latter action more or less brought the NWICO movement to a close, even though during the early 1990s many observers hoped that it would make a comeback. While accomplishing a lot intellectually in terms of collecting data on information imbalances, few actual agreements were reached.

The immediate international demand at this point consisted of the developing world trying to regulate journalistic activities, which was reflected in the 1978 mass media declaration. It represented the first attempt to provide guidelines for journalists working in the developing world. The UNESCO Declaration on the Mass Media, as it came to be known, was introduced in 1970 by the Soviet Union and represented over eight years of negotiations. It was titled "The Declaration of Fundamental Principles Concerning the Contribution of the Mass Media to Strengthening Peace and International Understanding, to the Promotion of Human Rights and to Countering Racialism, Apartheid and Incitement to War." Attempts by developing countries to actually regulate the activities of media firms' activities within their borders were defeated because of pressure from Western nations.[20] Next, many developing countries sought to license and, therefore, reduce the number of journalists within their borders. Other conferences began to express similar concerns, including a conference of 30,000 journalists at Mexico City, which tried to propose a code for journalistic ethics. The issue flared up in 1981 when UNESCO sponsored a meeting on the protection of journalists, an issue of importance to many international journalist unions. Instead, the meeting's focus became governmental jurisdiction. The North accused the South of not only wanting to reduce numbers of foreign journalists but also of wanting to permit only government-blessed news stories.[21] Nothing but heated exchanges emerged from the meetings.

The MacBride Commission submitted its report in 1980 to the UNESCO General Conference in Belgrade and a couple of positive developments followed after the adoption of this report at the General Conference. Amidst the heated polemics of the other debates, the Commission's report was a sobering reflection on the needs of the developing world and was a clarion call for improvement of information infrastructures in these countries. It also called attention to the lack of communication technology (as opposed to merely flows) governing North–South communication relations. On the technology count, the West was more willing to help. Accordingly, at the initiative of the United States, the International Programme for the Development of Communication (IPDC) was established, which would, among other things, look into transfers of technology. The program languished because of lack of funding and after the United States, and the United Kingdom pulled out of UNESCO, it all but died.

NWICO concerns also spilled over into other UN organizations. At the World Administrative Radio Conferences (WARCs) sponsored by the International Telecommunications Union, questions regarding the sovereignty of the developing country states vis-à-vis satellite broadcasts were raised. Of particular concern were direct broadcasting satellites (DBS) which would broadcast directly to homes. Many developing countries found this unacceptable. Here, they also had the support of many West European governments who were seeking to preserve their national markets. Therefore, the principle governing television broadcasts that emerged from the successive WARCs was that television broadcasts would be limited to national markets.

After the publication of the MacBride Commission report, the establishment of the IPDC, and the perceived futility of the heated arguments at the 1980 UNESCO General Conference, there was indication that UNESCO might enter a more "pragmatic" phase. In fact, the shift in focus to the need to enhance communication infrastructures rather than communication flows would be an enduring legacy of the MacBride report. However, just as this was beginning to happen, the entire NWICO movement lost its momentum due to political developments in the West.

Margaret Thatcher and Ronald Reagan would find UNESCO's demands to be unacceptable. The conservative constituencies supported Thatcher and Reagan, of course, but they also received support from the relatively independent or liberal media firms in their countries. Reagan's coming to office would be an especially welcome development. Reagan endorsed the Tuilleries Declaration from France in 1981 by the World Press Freedom Committee with delegates from 21 countries, which asked UNESCO to abandon its demands. In July 1981, Senator Danforth Quayle introduced a resolution in the US Senate for the United States to withdraw from UNESCO altogether. Meanwhile both mainstream media in the United States as well as conservative think-tanks like the Heritage Foundation attacked UNESCO. Perhaps due to ominous pressure from the West or because of the more practical influence of the work of the MacBride Commission, UNESCO's 1982–83 meetings were quite tame and focused mostly on communication technology issues. At the end of 1983, the United States withdrew from UNESCO. There was congressional and media support for the action. Soon after, the UK and Singapore followed suit. NWICO continued to be supported by UNESCO and NAM but it slowly fizzled out. UNESCO, which got 30 percent of its $200 million budget from the United States, could not sustain many of its efforts financially.[22] Many planned round tables on NWICO (such as the one organized in Igls, Austria, in 1983) were subsequently postponed or did not take place. In intellectual quarters, there was some talk that the NWICO concept might be revived when the European Union passed its TV directive seeking to control foreign (especially US) programming in 1989. The directive led to US and EU fights in the GATT and later WTO (see Chapter 4) but the NWICO issue was not revived. Federico Mayor, after becoming director-general of UNESCO in 1987, stopped supporting or promoting NWICO.

Toward knowledge societies

The MacBride Commission's report remains an enduring legacy of the NWICO era. Whatever its broad politics or specific recommendations, the intellectual heart of the report is the forceful consistency with which it makes the case for communication for a viable society. It questions the instrumental wisdom of merely providing infrastructures or access, and it broadens communication to beyond messages and information. It connects communication to people's everyday lives in terms of both material prosperity and human dignity. The first sentences of the report read: "Communication maintains and animates life. It is also the motor and expression of social activity and civilization ... "[23] The last paragraph closes thus:

> It is important to realize that the new order we seek is not only a goal but a stage in a journey. It is a continuing quest for ever more free, more equal, more just relations within all societies and among all nations and people. This Report represents what we believe we have learned. And, above all, we wish to communicate.[24]

After the NWICO debates ended and the communication sector was reorganized, it began to concentrate on issues that have been alternatively termed "the knowledge society" and "the information society." The communication sector has been somewhat timid after NWICO. "People are very conscious of that polarized thinking," said one UNESCO official.[25] The sector is continually asked to develop a code for journalistic ethics but the staff realize that they will not be able to get it through the UNESCO Executive Board. Nevertheless, the lessons from the MacBride Commission's report can be traced into these current global deliberations on the contours of an information society. The importance given to communication in the report offers as much guidance to a world in which there are social media and the Internet as it did at a time in 1980 when discussions tended to center around telecommunications and mass media.

UNESCO is now one of the international organizations in the World Summit for an Information Society (WSIS), which began in 1998 as an International Telecommunications Union initiative to examine digital divide issues. ITU asked the UN secretary-general to convene WSIS and received the authorization through the UN General Assembly's resolution 56/183. WSIS was also building upon "digital divide" issues that became prominent on the international agenda for several reasons. First, many countries liberalized their telecommunications infrastructures, ushering in private market players to replace public monopolies in telecommunications, broadcasting and, where they existed, in newspaper publishing. While a few countries leapfrogged, others were getting left behind. Second, the growth rates of infrastructural provision in many countries were enormous but these were unevenly distributed both in terms of infrastructure and the ability to communicate with it. Access to public policy assured large players and big metropolitan areas in developing countries that they would be provided with state-of-the-art communications, but rural areas and other marginalized groups were left behind. Studies even showed how new information and communication technologies came with either a gender bias or were appropriated by men in organizations. Third, to the extent that new technologies became available, transnational advocacy organizations proliferated and, in a twist of circumstances, brought further attention to the digital divide and the role of communication in human rights. Fourth, whereas the NWICO debate was confined to UNESCO and ITU, by the turn of the century just about every development organization was giving serious consideration to ideas of the information society and relevant technologies. Most international development organizations, both governmental and non-governmental, have projects dealing with ICTs. For example, Muhammad Yunus' innovative microfinance efforts through the Grameen bank, that garnered the Nobel Peace Prize in 2006, depend on the provision of mobile phones and sensitivity to gender roles in their utilization.

The World Summit on the Information Society (WSIS) began as a movement to consider information society ideas as broadly as possible.

WSIS deliberations included multiple stakeholders—businesses, governments, civil society, international organizations, experts—as part of a global movement toward what is being termed "mush," or multiple stakeholder diplomacy. The WSIS convened two major global summits apart from numerous other forums: in 2003 in Geneva and in 2005 in Tunis. One of the transnational civil society campaigns that made it to the Tunis agenda was the Communication Rights for an Information Society (CRIS) campaign. The campaign resulted from the Platform for Communication Rights, a worldwide group of civil society NGOs including the powerful Association for Progressive Communication (APC), working on communication issues. They received help not only from UNESCO deliberations but also from particular national commissions for UNESCO. For example, the World Association of Community Broadcasters (AMARC) met in May 2005 in Canada to discuss CRIS issues at the invitation of the Canadian National Commission for UNESCO.

UNESCO's communication and information sector had begun thinking along the lines of a knowledge society way before the WSIS processes began. It is therefore not surprising that the various official documents and declarations from the WSIS make several references to UNESCO's expertise and efforts. Box 5.1 lists the annex to the *Tunis Agenda for the Information Society* that resulted from the 2005 meetings.[26] This annex lists the action items and the lead organizations to implement these initiatives. In many ways the current priorities of the communication and information sector, or C&I as it is known in UNESCO, are organized around the action items defined for UNESCO in the Tunis Agenda. A listing of major C&I themes includes the following:

- information accessibility to all using traditional and new technologies;
- producing multi-media content to address cultural diversity;
- training ICT professionals to develop suitable infrastructures, especially for marginalized groups such as women; and
- emphasis on independent media organizations.

An information brochure from C&I summarizes UNESCO involvement as such:

> For the two phases of the World Summits on the Information Society (WSIS), in Geneva (Switzerland), December 2003 and Tunis (Tunisia) November 2005, UNESCO has elaborated the position that the Knowledge Society must be based on freedom of expression,

Box 5.1 Annex to the Tunis Agenda for the Information Society

Action Line	Possible moderators/facilitators
C1. The role of public governance authorities and all stakeholders in the promotion of ICTs for development	ECOSOC/UN Regional Commissions/ITU
C2. Information and communication infrastructure	ITU
C3. Access to information and knowledge	ITU/UNESCO
C4. Capacity building	UNDP/UNESCO/ITU/UNCTAD
C5. Building confidence and security in the use of ICTs	ITU
C6. Enabling environment	ITU/UNDP/UN REGIONAL COMMISSIONS/UNCTAD
C7. ICT Applications • E-government • E-business • E-learning • E-health • E-employment • E-environment • E-agriculture • E-Science	 • UNDP/ITU • WTO/UNCTAD/ITU/UPU • UNESCO/ITU/UNIDO • WHO/ITU • ILO/ITU • WHO/WMO/UNEP/UN-Habitat/ ITU/ICAO • FAO/ITU • UNESCO/ITU/UNTAD
C8. Cultural diversity and identity, linguistic diversity and local content	UNESCO
C9. Media	UNESCO
C10. Ethical dimensions of the Information Society	UNESCO/ECOSOC
C11. International and regional cooperation	UN Regional Commissions/ UNDP/ITU/UNESCO/ECOSOC

Source: http://www.itu.int/wsis/docs2/tunis/off/6rev1.html

access to information, cultural and linguistic diversity, and education opportunity for all with the use of ICTs. UNESCO will continue to play a leading role in following-up on these conferences.[27]

UNESCO's 2005 World Report, *Towards Knowledge Societies*, is also an endeavor placing the issues of the entire organization from lifelong education, to science, to indigenous knowledge as relevant for the creation of knowledge societies infused with information and communication networks.[28]

The WSIS, like any other global initiative, has its own politics that have also to some extent served to marginalize UNESCO. By the time of the 2005 Tunis summit, for example, Internet governance issues dominated the WSIS agenda. This was partly a result of the push given to Internet governance at ITU and the appointment of the UN secretary-general's Working Group on Internet Governance (WGIG). From its inception, WGIG was a high-profile group and attracted a great deal of opposition from the incumbent private player in internet governance, the Internet Corporation for Assigned Names and Numbers (ICANN), backed by the United States.[29] After the Tunis meeting, the Internet Governance Forum, which continues to convene meetings, picked up the Internet governance agenda. However, the net result was that Internet governance issues, rather than knowledge or information society issues, as broadly conceived earlier, began to dominate WSIS discussions after the 2003 Geneva summit.

Conclusion

UNESCO has made important contributions to global thinking regarding the importance of communication to society and to the international system. Whether or not one agrees with the politics of the issue, the fact that UNESCO, along with other organizations, has galvanized important stakeholders to deliberate the issues is in itself important. These discussions cannot be dismissed as "talking shops." If peace is built through understanding and insight into the minds of human beings, then the communication issues reveal a great deal about the human mind. UNESCO—more than the ITU, the World Bank, UNDP, or UNCTAD—is best situated to define communication issues in the broadest sense.

In moving forward on communication, UNESCO must deal with its own legacies. First, the NWICO agenda discredited the organization. In forging a communication agenda, UNESCO would need the help of media organizations and countries like the United States that it alienated. Second, it would need to let go of ideological baggage. Many intellectuals and experts continue to chant the vices of the market system like a mantra despite the fact that the proliferation of new technologies and their effective use even at the grassroots level has a great deal to do with the falling marginal costs of technology deployment. The legacy of the early thinking against markets may be hard to overcome but at the very least the premises need to be questioned with new evidence.[30] This may be a place for UNESCO to start and to engage civil society, corporate players (through the global compact), and states. More recently, UNESCO has begun to sign agreements with private enterprises. In the communication and information sector, partnerships include those with Expedia, Google, Microsoft, and Hewlett-Packard. For an organization that was fighting capitalism less than a generation ago, these partnerships have been "like throwing a hand grenade" into the organization.[31]

There is broad acceptance within the secretariat that in the twenty-first century communication issues need to be viewed from different perspectives. The following passage from Gabriel Garcia Marquez and Juan Somavia, members of the MacBride Commission, remains relevant:

> Communication is not just news. It is a determining factor of all social processes and a fundamental component of the way societies are organized. This approach taken by the report permits a more ample and balanced understanding of the problems involved and gives individual issues a more global perspective. This will allow the international debate on communications to be set in its proper overall political, economic and cultural context.[32]

6 Reflections and possibilities

Bernard: "Commissioner, can I introduce you to Missour Belroget from UNESCO?"
Commissioner: "UNESCO, ah yes gallant little country."
From "A Diplomatic Incident," BBC TV Sitcom *Yes Minister*

There is something about UNESCO that is so quixotic—moral adventures, high idealism, lofty humanism, intellectual guideposts, ethical monumentalism, worldwide deeds and, above all, its quest to shape human solidarity. This is the best of UNESCO. At its worst, well, UNESCO is hardly understood; it remains little known, as in the Commissioner's ignorance, as a gallant little country. UNESCO's ministers themselves often fail to rise to the occasion of their organization's ideals. Instead, they fight over meager resources, politicize their ideals, remain inefficient and nepotistic, and claim a stake to every one of humanity's problems from flows of communication in the skies above, to primary school education on earth, to the analysis of minerals below its surface. All that UNESCO does for a $300 million annual regular budget and a staff of 2,000.

How relevant is UNESCO to global governance as a shared ideal? The answer obviously depends on who takes part in UNESCO, how much gets shared, and where global governance is headed. This chapter analyzes this question in three parts, starting with the origins and creation of UNESCO's vision, an analysis of its everyday practices, and the future challenges it faces. Viewed from these perspectives, UNESCO's strengths and achievements are a microcosm of those of the United Nations system. Its visionary founders rose above the rubble of a devastating war to create an organization that was perhaps too idealistic, but to not have created one would have been worse. To the question, how far have we come with a United Nations or UNESCO, the answer must also take an account of the "we." Who are we now? Are we nations, ethnicities, social networks, markets, civil societies, individuals, or governments? All of the above?

A reality check is also necessary. UNESCO, like the UN, is too underfunded to ever achieve the high ideals placed at its door. Relatively speaking though, UNESCO remains among the top three to four of the UN specialized agencies in terms of resources (Table 1.5). Each year, it has the capacity to more than double its resources through extra-budgetary contributions. It can raise more from burgeoning initiatives such as Kofi Annan's global compact that allows the UN to partner with businesses and civil society. UNESCO's secretariat is not limited to 2,000 people either. From the diplomatic missions attached to UNESCO, to the National Commissions in member states, to the vast networks of intellectuals, schools, institutes, and NGOs affiliated with UNESCO, the organization has a capacity that ranks it among the top hierarchies of global governors. These concluding reflections on UNESCO as an organization, therefore, also take their cues from this reality check, and note that UNESCO has under-delivered on its resources and that it can do better.

UNESCO's vision

UNESCO's foremost vision about the world seeks to construct "the defences of peace" in "the minds of men." Spanish educator Ramón-Luis Acuña, writing in *Le Monde Diplomatique*, paraphrased this vision as: "Citizens of the world, stop killing each other."[1] Neither the depth of the original vision, nor its apparent lightness in the paraphrasing, takes away from its high-mindedness. It speaks to UNESCO's sense of moral purpose that, but for a handful of detractors, few critique this vision as unnecessary or irrelevant while many stop to reflect on it. It is in these reflections that UNESCO has added the most to global values of peace and will continue to do so. UNESCO's Preamble "is a religion here," noted one UNESCO official, "everyone believes it."[2]

Imagine the world of 1945. The Germans surrender on 8 May and the Japanese on 15 August, and there are nearly 75 million casualties. The United Nations project is guided by delegates who "were motivated by their reaction to the horrors and destruction of World War II but also by a determination not to repeat the economic difficulties that had led to the Great Depression of the 1930s. While the UN was not originally conceived of as a world government, nonetheless it also was not the creation of pie-in-the-sky idealists."[3]

There was a draft of the UNESCO constitution in circulation by April 1945, and in November 1945 UNESCO would come into being. The delegates were not misled, they were practical, and also truly visionary. Richard Cowell, former secretary-general of the British National Commission, provides an engrossing account of the 1945 Drafting Committee that met on "a cold November morning in a small unheated room."[4] Throughout 1945, education delegates and others recounted the horrors of the war and responded to the United Nations Information Organization's *Allied Plan for Education*, which articulated the concerns of the core CAME countries.

> Dr Falski of Poland told the most tragic tale of all: one seventh of the children of Poland between the ages of eight and fourteen had died, hardly one single Jewish child remained alive, a quarter of Poland's teachers were missing together with about 350 of Poland's University teachers. All the equipment of the schools of trade and technology with half Poland's art treasures had been carried away or destroyed. There were no books and the children lacked shoes. No more than about 3,000 of Poland's doctors remained to cope with a sickness rate among children fifteen times greater than it had been before the war.[5]

The people who framed UNESCO's ideals acknowledged the reality of the world they were operating in: "the early deliberations of the Conference of Allied Ministers of Education were dominated by very definite practical worries and material needs."[6] They were also visionaries and that's how we remember them: from the United States, Senator William Fulbright of Arkansas, and the poet Archibald Macleish; from the United Kingdom, education ministers Richard Butler and Ellen Wilkinson, Nancy Parkinson from the British Council, the humanist Julian Huxley, scientist Joseph Needham; from France, stalwart statesmen and leaders such as Leon Blum, Henri Bonnet, René Cassin, André Malraux, and Jacques Maritain; from Mexico came Jaime Torres Bodet who became UNESCO's second director-general. India's philosopher, and later the country's president, Sarvepalli Radhakrishnan, noted at the first General Conference in 1946 something that resonates with the credo of post-colonial writings that guided UNESCO's pedagogies later: "We must give the disinherited people the breath of an everlasting spirit, the sense of a liberating faith, which is distinct from the intellectual narrowness and rigidity of revelatory creeds which would accept no standards as valid save the explicit prescription of canonical texts."[7] Views such as Radhakrishnan's foreshadowed the

North–South debates that followed two decades later: in 1946, though, while there were disagreements, everyone agreed that these should be resolved through international organizations such as UNESCO. UNESCO's vision and its underlying practical necessities are understandable. The difficult thing for UNESCO's torchbearers—be they member states or intellectuals—is in coming up with a set of values that can translate this vision into practice. Thus, James Sewell notes in the context of UNESCO: "International organizations' charters proclaim a better future for mankind; yet, unavoidably, their human participants live in this world."[8] UNESCO's intellectual and political processes have not always delivered resoundingly positive results and UNESCO is often playing catch-up with social transformations and intellectual trends. In a recent interview, the new director-general, Irina Bokova, noted: "The concept of peace is no longer the same."[9] We also do not quite know how the minds of human beings work toward peace. Reinhold Niebuhr had doubted in the 1940s that education by itself could make human beings stop killing each other. UNESCO has similarly oscillated between encouraging high Kantian idealism and curbing stark Hobbesian pessimism regarding human nature.

UNESCO's deliberative capacities were perhaps best adapted from the Paris-based International Institute for Intellectual Cooperation (IIIC). Conceived as such, and fashioned in the cultural traditions of the French intellectuals, this precedent led UNESCO to view itself as the intellectual laboratory of the world. The French had in fact wanted the agency to be led by such intellectuals and civil society. The first tension in UNESCO's vision lies here: intellectual traditions shape its agenda and vision but politics must then translate them into results.

What intellectuals suggest, politics often does not follow. Julian Huxley was idealistic but practical and cautioned the United States against politicizing UNESCO's agenda with respect to the Soviets. The United States would have nothing of such slowness and pushed forward a program of media freedoms and information that led to the withdrawal of Eastern bloc countries and the Soviet refusal to join the organization. Later, in 1980, the MacBride Commission Report was a visionary reflection on the importance of communication to the human species. Nobel Peace Laureate Sean MacBride was a tireless legal advocate of human rights. In the hands of radical crusaders from the Eastern bloc and the developing world, the MacBride Commission's recommendations were forgotten in favor of scathing critiques of the Western world's media practices. The United States itself misunderstood that government control of media is not always harmful—from the BBC in the United Kingdom to the lack of private enterprises in disseminating news and information in the developing world, the government was often also involved in resolving a public goods problem. Similarly, the lessons of Javier Pérez de Cuéllar's World Commission of Culture and Development were lost in the fight between a French-Canadian led coalition of mostly film and television activists versus Hollywood. It is in fact amazing that UNESCO's politics succeeded in vitiating the report *Our Creative Diversity*'s lessons to apply solely to trade and culture conflicts while they were originally intended to apply chiefly to the developing world. There have, of course, been other reports that could not be politicized but were hard to translate into any kind of practice. The Delors Commission's *Learning: The Treasure Within* is one such instance. Nevertheless, the report is important in putting the concept of education in the context of human dignity rather than merely instrumental survival or material gain.

Two problems are paramount to an organization that views itself as an intellectual laboratory. First, if "the minds of men" are intellectual minds, then can they speak for the world's vast humanity? UNESCO's coffers are full of commission reports and expert group documents from the minds of the well-educated luminaries and political leadership of the world. This is an elite vision of the world and ready to be exploited for various political expediencies. The second related issue is who listens to this vision? UNESCO spends a great deal of time and resources producing various iterations of its education, science, communication, and culture ideals but much less on connecting them to the everyday world of practice. This is not just a question of information dissemination but a fundamental structural flaw in the organization. Contrast this with the think-tanks of Washington, DC, which spend a great deal of time aligning themselves with political processes and institutions. Perhaps, it would be difficult for UNESCO to be a Brookings, or a Carnegie, and definitely not a Heritage Foundation (which remains UNESCO's nemesis), but if UNESCO is to be an intellectual think-tank, it needs to accord serious attention to boosting its organizational capacities to lead politics rather than be led by them.

There is another legacy of being an intellectually driven organization and providing cultural solutions to bring peace to the world. A cultural approach, at least in the twenty-first century, must engage people's minds and not just intellectual minds in its processes. That people have a mind of their own sounds brusque. But when UNESCO says "minds of men," whose minds are being consulted in its decision-making? Generally, UNESCO reaches out to the intellectual elite. One memoir in 1986 from a UNESCO social and human sciences official who had been with the organization for over 30 years noted:

When I look back on the hours and hours I spent listening to experts who had never actually dealt with a juvenile delinquent, never had been party to the negotiation of a labor dispute, never tried to cope with problems of a mother of eleven in a favella or the dilemmas of small businesses in precarious situations talking airily about applied social science I must wonder where I have been these thirty years.[10]

Our Creative Diversity suggests cultural participation and empowerment can overcome structural barriers to democracy, such as poverty and segregation. This is not a top-down approach. The first task of UNESCO must then be to broaden the deliberative processes that would build the defenses of peace in the minds of human beings.

It seems fairly certain now, as it was in 1945, that the question of positive peace would need to be explored at the cultural level. After noting that the concept of peace is no longer the same, Irina Bokova, in the interview cited above, continued that "it is tolerance and respect for others that matter. The world has become a multipolar place; more democratic, more dynamic too. And I think our time has come."[11] If it has, then it must engage effectively with this multipolar and democratic world. A top-down intellectual approach is advisable only if it is cognizant of bottom-up processes. The report *What UNESCO for the Future* delineates what UNESCO can and should do in the future and its words come from the world's finest minds—Jacques Attali, Boutros Boutros-Ghali, Hisahi Owada, and many others. Embedded in these pages are ideas of values and cooperation but also a sense of the process that must make attaining UNESCO's ideals possible. For better or for worse, human solidarity will need to take account of the differences between human beings to fashion solutions of peace. Harvard academic Tu Weiming notes in this report: "Without different sounds, there is no music. Without different colors, there are no paintings. Geodiversity and biodiversity are preconditions for human survival and linguistic and cultural diversity is congenial to human suffering."[12]

It is unclear if UNESCO, the United Nations, or global humanity has figured out the ideal way to paint or make music. However, what's more important is that organizations like UNESCO can keep alive the processes and indulge humanity in their endeavors to design or implement these ideals. To borrow from Paulo Freire's words, UNESCO as a pedagogic organization would be better off in keeping alive the value of problem-solving humanity's toughest issues through dialogues. This would contrast with what Freire would call an embankment approach that provides ready-made monologic solutions that humanity feels uncomfortable accepting. Recent writers have begun to refer to the "Third UN" as important for global governance.[13] The first two UNs, as Inis Claude's famous treatise pointed out, dealt respectively with the member states and the secretariats that implemented their prerogatives.[14] The Third UN consists of the civil society, individuals, experts, and academics that now fashion global governance processes. In 1946, UNESCO moved forward as an intellectual organization led by member states. It needs to revisit this compact now in the context of the Third UN.

Everyday practices

Accounts of UNESCO tend to be as critical of the member state driven politics of UNESCO, the first UN, as they are of its secretariat, the second UN. The previous section summarized to some extent where the first UN has failed and how the third UN needs to be brought in. This section details the critiques of the "Second UN" or the inner functioning of the secretariat at UNESCO.

When President George W. Bush and the US Congress began to inch toward rejoining UNESCO 10 years ago, UNESCO's conservative critics in the country were quick to seize the opportunity to denounce the $60–70 million bill that the United States would have to afford for an organization that remained corrupt, inefficient, overly bureaucratic, nepotistic, inefficient, incompetent and, above all, anti-American.[15] Nevertheless, the somewhat exaggerated critiques from the United States of UNESCO's inner functioning do find some resonance in the various audits and stocktakings of UNESCO as an organization.

UNESCO's critiques also require some perspective. Organizational dynamics like the ones mentioned in the last paragraph are not unique to UNESCO alone. While a few corruption stories at UNESCO are legendary—Senegal's Mahatar M'Bow awarding top posts to his relatives or, more recently, ex-US Congressman Peter Smith awarding lucrative education contracts to his favored firm in Chicago when he was ADG of education—corruption is also the stuff of politics everywhere. This is not a case for overlooking corruption, but one for providing a perspective on its scope. Ex-director-general Koïchiro Matsuura, credited with cleaning up UNESCO's hiring and organizational practices, is also himself blamed in a few accounts for producing a culture of cronyism and authoritarian methods.[16] Sometimes it is also a matter of conflicting perspectives.

Reform might come from the same players who might otherwise be viewed as high-minded or arrogant. DG Maheu was known to be supercilious and occasionally driven to fits of anger but he is also praised for his hard work and vision. DG Matsuura is widely credited with initiating processes at UNESCO that have led to considerable house cleaning and created systems of accountability at various levels of hiring practices, reducing waste in the organization, and monitoring goals that the sectors set for themselves. The United States sees inefficiency and corruption everywhere, while often turning a blind eye to the corruption within its own borders. Nevertheless, it also has an excellent record for efficiency and accountability. In this sense the re-entry of the United States may be good for UNESCO.

Beyond the organizational culture that UNESCO sustains within, there is the question of the secretariat's outputs. The rivalries and competitiveness within its sectors are surely lamentable, but short of a transformative restructuring, these rivalries will continue, and by themselves might even account for a modicum of efficiency induced through competition over scarce resources. Nevertheless, intersectoral cooperation remains a daunting challenge for UNESCO. One of the problems with getting sectors to cooperate is that UNESCO's agenda-setting is broad and vague.[17] This allows the sectors to propose myriad programs that suit their immediate interests, or those of the member states pushing for them, rather than truly fashioning an intersectoral approach. "Gender" or "Africa" or "culture of peace" as intersectoral priorities may not mean much if each sector merely does what it wants to do with dissecting them rather than fashioning a common approach and a shared set of achievable goals. UNESCO's strategic planners are well aware that accountability vertically within a sector is hard enough; it may be near impossible across sectors.[18]

Agenda-setting as a whole for UNESCO has been hard. Constructing defenses of peace in the minds of human beings has led to a proliferation of hundreds of highly ambitious and laudable initiatives. Whichever way UNESCO's capacity is viewed—an organization with a staff of 2,000 and a regular budget of $500 million, or with $1 billion and vast networks—a hundred initiatives is unmanageable. Furthermore, as Richard Hoggart notes, it is hard for an organization to effectively indulge in program implementation when it is always playing catch-up to its six-monthly Executive Board, biennial General Conference meetings, and the convoluted budgetary allocation processes, which translate its agenda into practice.[19] As Chapter 1 noted, competition for budgetary resources and allocation consume a great deal of time and energy within sectors. Every international organization faces a dilemma between its secretariat's internal prerogatives and the need for its staffers to interact with the rest of the world, especially in home countries, to implement the initiatives designed at the headquarters. UNESCO is moving toward decentralizing the organization—one-half of its staff is now in its 58 field offices—but it also needs to streamline the number of initiatives it can take up. Furthermore, unlike country directors at the World Bank who have control over their budgets, most of the budgetary decisions for the UNESCO field offices are made in Paris.

The successes of UNESCO's secretariat are in areas where its initiatives were adopted at the national or sub-national levels. This volume has recounted the success of the World Heritage program, national science policy organizations, the Sourcebook for Science, and calculations of educational goals from around the world by involving education ministries and schools. In all these cases, UNESCO staff worked closely with the national and sub-national organizations. However, UNESCO is still considerably limited in field operations—1,000 staff in over 50 field offices. These staff must then figure how best to interact with governmental and non-governmental officials in implementing their programs in their respective regions. While there are numerous critiques of these implementations, their successes feature some calibration between secretariat capacity and resources and the societal needs. This does not mean that UNESCO should stop deliberating bioethics, globalization complexities, or cultures of peace. It only means narrowing down the initiatives to manageable intersectoral projects that can be connected with the networks that must be galvanized for their implementation.

Future challenges

I have suggested above that UNESCO is best suited for broadening the processes of deliberation and dialogue that forge global values for peace. Further, in order to work effectively, UNESCO will need to streamline its agenda. The third part of UNESCO's challenge lies in the complexity of its future challenges. By any account, globalization continues to increase the intensity of its interactions, the extent of the issues it covers, the velocity with which it unfolds, and its impact on everyday and institutional life.[20] Not only is the world multipolar but also the technologies of its transformation continue to add layers of complexity and immediacy. In an introduction to the seminal report *The Computerization of Society*, that awoke France's government to prioritizing information technologies in the 1970s, the sociologist Daniel Bell foretold of positive possibilities but also the negative fallout from coming technologies:[21]

But information differs from electricity in the obvious sense that people react to information, and the enlargement of scale ties the entire world together more quickly, and creates more volatile situations, than at any other time in human history.

Given the promise and the volatility in this world of new technologies and interactions, it is important to remember that we have global institutions that can help us deliberate and problem-solve complex issues. This view regarding institutional path dependence is shared widely in various types of scholarship. James Rosenau wrote that global governance is as much about institutions and formal charters as it is about intersubjective conceptions.[22] Neo-institutionalist conceptions of global governance continue to show that once institutions are founded, they have a life of their own, regardless of the demise of the original processes that created them. More recent scholarship calls attention to the life of these institutions, including the Routledge series to which this volume belongs, but also to the governors themselves and the intersubjective and abstract ways in which this global governance is apprehended. Bringing in the third UN or multiple stakeholders to bear upon these institutions is also no longer a choice. From the World Social Forum to the World Summit on the Information Society, the third UN and multistakeholderism are already there. In other words, in tackling global complexity, it is useful to remember that we may not have the solutions but that we have the global institutions and the intersubjective conceptions of global governance shared around the world. To his own question, "Should UNESCO survive?", Richard Hoggart answers that the organization "is worth saving precisely because it has a Constitution which calls it to activities beyond technical cooperation."[23] Toward the end of his concluding chapter to the book, he notes, "UNESCO was founded on the idea of an appeal to the sense of a common suffering mankind reduced by a long war and determined to build a fairer world. In its origins it has more in common with the universe of King Lear than with that of Machiavelli, and should not be allowed to forget it."[24]

UNESCO's sense of moral purpose is its enduring strength. "The Preamble sends chills up and down the spine," says one UNESCO official—"how prescient that if we believe in knowledge and implementation in five domains, we can stop killing each other."[25] As an important global institution, UNESCO has enormous intellectual capabilities to deliberate the most complex of global problems related to constructing the defenses of peace in the minds of human beings. Broadening such processes, despite the Machiavellian maneuvering of its member states or their representatives in Paris, bodes well for the future of global governance understood as multilateral problem-solving and dialogues.

Appendix
UNESCO Constitution

The constitution of UNESCO, signed on 16 November 1945, came into force on 4 November 1946 after ratification by 20 countries: Australia, Brazil, Canada, China, Czechoslovakia, Denmark, Dominican Republic, Egypt, France, Greece, India, Lebanon, Mexico, New Zealand, Norway, Saudi Arabia, South Africa, Turkey, the United Kingdom, and the United States.

Constitution of the United Nations Educational, Scientific and Cultural Organization

Adopted in London on 16 November 1945 and amended by the General Conference at its 2nd, 3rd, 4th, 5th, 6th, 7th, 8th, 9th, 10th, 12th, 15th, 17th, 19th, 20th, 21st, 24th, 25th, 26th, 27th, 28th, 29th, and 31st sessions.

The Governments of the States Parties to this Constitution on behalf of their peoples declare:

That since wars begin in the minds of men, it is in the minds of men that the defences of peace must be constructed;

That ignorance of each other's ways and lives has been a common cause, throughout the history of mankind, of that suspicion and mistrust between the peoples of the world through which their differences have all too often broken into war;

That the great and terrible war which has now ended was a war made possible by the denial of the democratic principles of the dignity, equality and mutual respect of men, and by the propagation, in their place, through ignorance and prejudice, of the doctrine of the inequality of men and races;

That the wide diffusion of culture, and the education of humanity for justice and liberty and peace are indispensable to the dignity of man and constitute a sacred duty which all the nations must fulfil in a spirit of mutual assistance and concern;

That a peace based exclusively upon the political and economic arrangements of governments would not be a peace which could secure the unanimous, lasting and sincere support of the peoples of the world, and that the peace must therefore be founded, if it is not to fail, upon the intellectual and moral solidarity of mankind.

For these reasons, the States Parties to this Constitution, believing in full and equal opportunities for education for all, in the unrestricted pursuit of objective truth, and in the free exchange of ideas and knowledge, are agreed and determined to develop and to increase the means of communication between their peoples and to employ these means for the purposes of mutual understanding and a truer and more perfect knowledge of each other's lives;

In consequence whereof they do hereby create the United Nations Educational, Scientific and Cultural Organization for the purpose of advancing, through the educational and scientific and cultural relations of the peoples of the world, the objectives of international peace and of the common welfare of mankind for which the United Nations Organization was established and which its Charter proclaims.

Article I

Purposes and functions

1. The purpose of the Organization is to contribute to peace and security by promoting collaboration among the nations through education, science and culture in order to further universal respect for justice, for the rule of law and for the human rights and fundamental freedoms which are affirmed for the peoples of the world, without distinction of race, sex, language or religion, by the Charter of the United Nations.

2. To realize this purpose the Organization will:

(a) Collaborate in the work of advancing the mutual knowledge and understanding of peoples, through all means of mass communication and to that end recommend such international agreements as may be necessary to promote the free flow of ideas by word and image;

(b) Give fresh impulse to popular education and to the spread of culture:

By collaborating with Members, at their request, in the development of educational activities;

By instituting collaboration among the nations to advance the ideal of equality of educational opportunity without regard to race, sex or any distinctions, economic or social;

By suggesting educational methods best suited to prepare the children of the world for the responsibilities of freedom;

(c) Maintain, increase and diffuse knowledge:
By assuring the conservation and protection of the world's inheritance of books, works of art and monuments of history and science, and recommending to the nations concerned the necessary international conventions;
By encouraging cooperation among the nations in all branches of intellectual activity, including the international exchange of persons active in the fields of education, science and culture and the exchange of publications, objects of artistic and scientific interest and other materials of information;
By initiating methods of international cooperation calculated to give the people of all countries access to the printed and published materials produced by any of them.

3. With a view to preserving the independence, integrity and fruitful diversity of the cultures and educational systems of the States Members of the Organization, the Organization is prohibited from intervening in matters which are essentially within their domestic jurisdiction.

Article II

Membership

1. Membership of the United Nations Organization shall carry with it the right to membership of the United Nations Educational, Scientific and Cultural Organization.
2. Subject to the conditions of the Agreement between this Organization and the United Nations Organization, approved pursuant to Article X of this Constitution, states not members of the United Nations Organization may be admitted to membership of the Organization, upon recommendation of the Executive Board, by a two-thirds majority vote of the General Conference.
3. Territories or groups of territories which are not responsible for the conduct of their international relations may be admitted as Associate Members by the General Conference by a two-thirds majority of Members present and voting, upon application made on behalf of such territory or group of territories by the Member or other authority having responsibility for their international relations. The nature and extent of the rights and obligations of Associate Members shall be determined by the General Conference.
4. Members of the Organization which are suspended from the exercise of the rights and privileges of membership of the United Nations

Organization shall, upon the request of the latter, be suspended from the rights and privileges of this Organization.

5. Members of the Organization which are expelled from the United Nations Organization shall automatically cease to be Members of this Organization.

6. Any Member State or Associate Member of the Organization may withdraw from the Organization by notice addressed to the Director-General. Such notice shall take effect on 31 December of the year following that during which the notice was given. No such withdrawal shall affect the financial obligations owed to the Organization on the date the withdrawal takes effect. Notice of withdrawal by an Associate Member shall be given on its behalf by the Member State or other authority having responsibility for its international relations.

7. Each Member State is entitled to appoint a Permanent Delegate to the Organization.

8. The Permanent Delegate of the Member State shall present his credentials to the Director-General of the Organization, and shall officially assume his duties from the day of presentation of his credentials.

Article III

Organs

The Organization shall include a General Conference, an Executive Board and a Secretariat.

Article IV

The General Conference

A. COMPOSITION

1. The General Conference shall consist of the representatives of the States Members of the Organization. The Government of each Member State shall appoint not more than five delegates, who shall be selected after consultation with the National Commission, if established, or with educational, scientific and cultural bodies.

B. FUNCTIONS

2. The General Conference shall determine the policies and the main lines of work of the Organization. It shall take decisions on programmes submitted to it by the Executive Board.

3. The General Conference shall, when it deems desirable and in accordance with the regulations to be made by it, summon international conferences of states on education, the sciences and humanities or the dissemination of knowledge; non-governmental conferences on the same subjects may be summoned by the General Conference or by the Executive Board in accordance with such regulations.

4. The General Conference shall, in adopting proposals for submission to the Member States, distinguish between recommendations and international conventions submitted for their approval. In the former case a majority vote shall suffice; in the latter case a two-thirds majority shall be required. Each of the Member States shall submit recommendations or conventions to its competent authorities within a period of one year from the close of the session of the General Conference at which they were adopted.

5. Subject to the provisions of Article V, paragraph 6 (c), the General Conference shall advise the United Nations Organization on the educational, scientific and cultural aspects of matters of concern to the latter, in accordance with the terms and procedure agreed upon between the appropriate authorities of the two Organizations.

6. The General Conference shall receive and consider the reports sent to the Organization by Member States on the action taken upon the recommendations and conventions referred to in paragraph 4 above or, if it so decides, analytical summaries of these reports.

7. The General Conference shall elect the members of the Executive Board and, on the recommendation of the Board, shall appoint the Director-General.

C. VOTING

8. (a) Each Member State shall have one vote in the General Conference. Decisions shall be made by a simple majority except in cases in which a two-thirds majority is required by the provisions of this Constitution, or the Rules of Procedure of the General Conference. A majority shall be a majority of the Members present and voting.

(b) A Member State shall have no vote in the General Conference if the total amount of contributions due from it exceeds the total amount of contributions payable by it for the current year and the immediately preceding calendar year.

(c) The General Conference may nevertheless permit such a Member State to vote, if it is satisfied that failure to pay is due to conditions beyond the control of the Member State.

D. PROCEDURE

9. (a) The General Conference shall meet in ordinary session every two years. It may meet in extraordinary session if it decides to do so itself or if summoned by the Executive Board, or on the demand of at least one-third of the Member States.

(b) At each session the location of its next ordinary session shall be designated by the General Conference. The location of an extraordinary session shall be decided by the General Conference if the session is summoned by it, or otherwise by the Executive Board.

10. The General Conference shall adopt its own rules of procedure. It shall at each session elect a President and other officers.

11. The General Conference shall set up special and technical committees and such other subsidiary organs as may be necessary for its purposes.

12. The General Conference shall cause arrangements to be made for public access to meetings, subject to such regulations as it shall prescribe.

E. OBSERVERS

13. The General Conference, on the recommendation of the Executive Board and by a two-thirds majority may, subject to its rules of procedure, invite as observers at specified sessions of the Conference or of its commissions representatives of international organizations, such as those referred to in Article XI, paragraph 4.

14. When consultative arrangements have been approved by the Executive Board for such international non-governmental or semi-governmental organizations in the manner provided in Article XI, paragraph 4, those organizations shall be invited to send observers to sessions of the General Conference and its commissions.

Article V

Executive Board

A. COMPOSITION

1. (a) The Executive Board shall be elected by the General Conference and it shall consist of fifty-eight Member States. The President of the General Conference shall sit ex officio in an advisory capacity on the Executive Board.

(b) Elected States Members of the Executive Board are hereinafter referred to as "Members" of the Executive Board.

2. (a) Each Member of the Executive Board shall appoint one representative. It may also appoint alternates.

(b) In selecting its representative on the Executive Board, the Member of the Executive Board shall endeavour to appoint a person qualified in one or more of the fields of competence of UNESCO and with the necessary experience and capacity to fulfil the administrative and executive duties of the Board. Bearing in mind the importance of continuity, each representative shall be appointed for the duration of the term of the Member of the Executive Board, unless exceptional circumstances warrant his replacement. The alternates appointed by each Member of the Executive Board shall act in the absence of its representative in all his functions.

3. In electing Members to the Executive Board, the General Conference shall have regard to the diversity of cultures and a balanced geographical distribution.

4. (a) Members of the Executive Board shall serve from the close of the session of the General Conference which elected them until the close of the second ordinary session of the General Conference following their election. The General Conference shall, at each of its ordinary sessions, elect the number of Members of the Executive Board required to fill vacancies occurring at the end of the session.

(b) Members of the Executive Board are eligible for re-election. Re-elected Members of the Executive Board shall endeavour to change their representatives on the Board.

5. In the event of the withdrawal from the Organization of a Member of the Executive Board, its term of office shall be terminated on the date when the withdrawal becomes effective.

B. FUNCTIONS

6. (a) The Executive Board shall prepare the agenda for the General Conference. It shall examine the programme of work for the Organization and corresponding budget estimates submitted to it by the Director-General in accordance with paragraph 3 of Article VI and shall submit them with such recommendations as it considers desirable to the General Conference.

(b) The Executive Board, acting under the authority of the General Conference, shall be responsible for the execution of the programme adopted by the Conference. In accordance with the decisions of the General Conference and having regard to circumstances arising between two ordinary sessions, the Executive Board shall take all necessary measures to ensure the effective and rational execution of the programme by the Director-General.

(c) Between ordinary sessions of the General Conference, the Board may discharge the functions of adviser to the United Nations, set forth in Article IV, paragraph 5, whenever the problem upon which advice is sought has already been dealt with in principle by the Conference, or when the solution is implicit in decisions of the Conference.

7. The Executive Board shall recommend to the General Conference the admission of new Members to the Organization.

8. Subject to decisions of the General Conference, the Executive Board shall adopt its own rules of procedure. It shall elect its officers from among its Members.

9. The Executive Board shall meet in regular session at least four times during a biennium and may meet in special session if convoked by the Chairman on his initiative or upon the request of six Members of the Executive Board.

10. The Chairman of the Executive Board shall present, on behalf of the Board, to the General Conference at each ordinary session, with or without comments, the reports on the activities of the Organization which the Director-General is required to prepare in accordance with the provisions of Article VI.3 (b).

11. The Executive Board shall make all necessary arrangements to consult the representatives of international organizations or qualified persons concerned with questions within its competence.

12. Between sessions of the General Conference, the Executive Board may request advisory opinions from the International Court of Justice on legal questions arising within the field of the Organization's activities.

13. The Executive Board shall also exercise the powers delegated to it by the General Conference on behalf of the Conference as a whole.

Article VI

Secretariat

1. The Secretariat shall consist of a Director-General and such staff as may be required.

2. The Director-General shall be nominated by the Executive Board and appointed by the General Conference for a period of four years, under such conditions as the Conference may approve. The Director-General may be appointed for a further term of four years but shall not be eligible for reappointment for a subsequent term. The Director-General shall be the chief administrative officer of the Organization.

3. (a) The Director-General, or a deputy designated by him, shall participate, without the right to vote, in all meetings of the General

Conference, of the Executive Board, and of the Committees of the Organization. He shall formulate proposals for appropriate action by the Conference and the Board, and shall prepare for submission to the Board a draft programme of work for the Organization with corresponding budget estimates.

(b) The Director-General shall prepare and communicate to Member States and to the Executive Board periodical reports on the activities of the Organization. The General Conference shall determine the periods to be covered by these reports.

4. The Director-General shall appoint the staff of the Secretariat in accordance with staff regulations to be approved by the General Conference. Subject to the paramount consideration of securing the highest standards of integrity, efficiency and technical competence, appointment to the staff shall be on as wide a geographical basis as possible.

5. The responsibilities of the Director-General and of the staff shall be exclusively international in character. In the discharge of their duties they shall not seek or receive instructions from any government or from any authority external to the Organization. They shall refrain from any action which might prejudice their positions as international officials. Each State Member of the Organization undertakes to respect the international character of the responsibilities of the Director-General and the staff, and not to seek to influence them in the discharge of their duties.

6. Nothing in this Article shall preclude the Organization from entering into special arrangements within the United Nations Organization for common services and staff and for the interchange of personnel.

Article VII

National cooperating bodies

1. Each Member State shall make such arrangements as suit its particular conditions for the purpose of associating its principal bodies interested in educational, scientific and cultural matters with the work of the Organization, preferably by the formation of a National Commission broadly representative of the government and such bodies.

2. National Commissions or National Cooperating Bodies, where they exist, shall act in an advisory capacity to their respective delegations to the General Conference, to the representatives and alternates of their countries on the Executive Board and to their Governments in matters relating to the Organization and shall function as agencies of liaison in all matters of interest to it.

3. The Organization may, on the request of a Member State, delegate, either temporarily or permanently, a member of its Secretariat to serve on the National Commission of that state, in order to assist in the development of its work.

Article VIII

Reports by Member States

Each Member State shall submit to the Organization, at such times and in such manner as shall be determined by the General Conference, reports on the laws, regulations and statistics relating to its educational, scientific and cultural institutions and activities, and on the action taken upon the recommendations and conventions referred to in Article IV, paragraph 4.

Article IX

Budget

1. The budget shall be administered by the Organization.
2. The General Conference shall approve and give final effect to the budget and to the apportionment of financial responsibility among the States Members of the Organization subject to such arrangement with the United Nations as may be provided in the agreement to be entered into pursuant to Article X.
3. The Director-General may accept voluntary contributions, gifts, bequests and subventions directly from governments, public and private institutions, associations and private persons, subject to the conditions specified in the Financial Regulations.

Article X

Relations with the United Nations Organization

This Organization shall be brought into relation with the United Nations Organization, as soon as practicable, as one of the specialized agencies referred to in Article 57 of the Charter of the United Nations. This relationship shall be effected through an agreement with the United Nations Organization under Article 63 of the Charter, which agreement shall be subject to the approval of the General Conference of this Organization. The agreement shall provide for effective cooperation between the two Organizations in the pursuit of their common purposes, and at the same time shall recognize the autonomy of this Organization, within the fields of its competence as defined in this Constitution. Such agreement may, among other matters, provide for the approval and financing of the budget of the Organization by the General Assembly of the United Nations.

Article XI

Relations with other specialized international organizations and agencies

1. This Organization may cooperate with other specialized intergovernmental organizations and agencies whose interests and activities are related to its purposes. To this end the Director-General, acting under the general authority of the Executive Board, may establish effective working relationships with such organizations and agencies and establish such joint committees as may be necessary to assure effective cooperation. Any formal arrangements entered into with such organizations or agencies shall be subject to the approval of the Executive Board.

2. Whenever the General Conference of this Organization and the competent authorities of any other specialized intergovernmental organizations or agencies whose purpose and functions lie within the competence of this Organization deem it desirable to effect a transfer of their resources and activities to this Organization, the Director-General, subject to the approval of the Conference, may enter into mutually acceptable arrangements for this purpose.

3. This Organization may make appropriate arrangements with other intergovernmental organizations for reciprocal representation at meetings.

4. The United Nations Educational, Scientific and Cultural Organization may make suitable arrangements for consultation and cooperation with non-governmental international organizations concerned with matters within its competence, and may invite them to undertake specific tasks. Such cooperation may also include appropriate participation by representatives of such organizations on advisory committees set up by the General Conference.

Article XII

Legal status of the Organization

The provisions of Articles 104 and 105 of the Charter of the United Nations Organization concerning the legal status of that Organization, its privileges and immunities, shall apply in the same way to this Organization.

Article XIII

Amendments

1. Proposals for amendments to this Constitution shall become effective upon receiving the approval of the General Conference by a two-thirds majority; provided, however, that those amendments which involve fundamental alterations in the aims of the Organization or new obligations for the Member States shall require subsequent acceptance on the part of two-thirds of the Member States before they come into force. The draft texts of proposed amendments shall be communicated by the Director-General to the Member States at least six months in advance of their consideration by the General Conference.

2. The General Conference shall have power to adopt by a two-thirds majority rules of procedure for carrying out the provisions of this Article.

Article XIV

Interpretation

1. The English and French texts of this Constitution shall be regarded as equally authoritative.

2. Any question or dispute concerning the interpretation of this Constitution shall be referred for determination to the International Court of Justice or to an arbitral tribunal, as the General Conference may determine under its Rules of Procedure.

Article XV

Entry into force

1. This Constitution shall be subject to acceptance. The instrument of acceptance shall be deposited with the Government of the United Kingdom.

2. This Constitution shall remain open for signature in the archives of the Government of the United Kingdom. Signature may take place either before or after the deposit of the instrument of acceptance. No acceptance shall be valid unless preceded or followed by signature.

However, a state that has withdrawn from the Organization shall simply deposit a new instrument of acceptance in order to resume membership.

3. This Constitution shall come into force when it has been accepted by twenty of its signatories. Subsequent acceptances shall take effect immediately.

4. The Government of the United Kingdom will inform all Members of the United Nations and the Director-General of the receipt of all instruments of acceptance and of the date on which the Constitution comes into force in accordance with the preceding paragraph.

In faith whereof, the undersigned, duly authorized to that effect, have signed this Constitution in the English and French languages, both texts being equally authentic.

Done in London the sixteenth day of November, one thousand nine hundred and forty-five, in a single copy, in the English and French languages, of which certified copies will be communicated by the Government of the United Kingdom to the Governments of all the Members of the United Nations.

Notes

Foreword

1 J. P. Singh's other authored books are: *Globalized Arts: The Entertainment Economy and Cultural Identity* (New York: Columbia University Press, 2011); *Negotiation and the Global Information Economy* (Cambridge: Cambridge University Press, 2008); and *Leapfrogging Development? The Political Economy of Telecommunications Restructuring* (Albany, N.Y.: State University of New York Press, 1999). His edited works are: *International Cultural Policies and Power* (Basingstoke, UK: Palgrave, 2010); and (with James N. Rosenau), *Information Technologies and Global Politics* (Albany, N.Y.: State University of New York Press, 2002).

Introduction

1 Julian Huxley, *UNESCO: Its Purpose and Its Philosophy* (Washington, DC: American Council of Public Affairs, 1947), 7.
2 Martha Finnemore and Kathryn Sikkink, "Norm Dynamics and Political Change," in Peter J. Katzenstein, Robert O. Keohane, and Stephen D. Krasner, eds., *Exploration and Contestation in the Study of World Politics* (Cambridge, Mass.: MIT Press, 2000), 251.
3 Antje Wiener, *The Invisible Constitution of Politics: Contested Norms and International Encounters* (Cambridge: Cambridge University Press, 2008).
4 Monsieur de Callières, *On the Manner of Negotiating with Princes; On the Uses of Diplomacy; the Choice of Ministers and Envoys; and the Personal Qualities Necessary for Success in Missions Abroad*, translated by A. F. White (Notre Dame, Ind.: University of Notre Dame Press, 1963 [1716]), 11.
5 Vincenzo Pavone, *From the Labyrinth of the World to the Paradise of the Heart: Science and Humanism in UNESCO's Approach to Globalization* (Lanham, Md.: Lexington Books, 2008), 34.
6 Quoted in Pavone, *From the Labyrinth of the World*, 140.
7 Quoted in Pavone, 141.
8 Huxley, *UNESCO*, 8.
9 American Humanist Association, "About Humanism" (available at: www.americanhumanist.org/Who_We_Are/About_Humanism/Humanist_Manifesto_I).
10 Roger-Pol Droit, *Humanity in the Making: Overview of the Intellectual History of the UNESCO 1945–2005* (Paris: UNESCO, 2005), 43.

11 Quoted in James P. Sewell, *UNESCO and World Politics: Engaging in International Relations* (Princeton, N.J.: Princeton University Press, 1975), 79.
12 Quoted in Sewell, *UNESCO*, 45.
13 Clare Wells, *The UN, UNESCO and the Politics of Knowledge* (New York: St. Martin's Press, 1987).
14 UNESCO World Report, *Investing in Cultural Diversity and Intercultural Dialogue* (Paris: UNESCO Publishing, 2009). Available at unesdoc.UNESCO. org/images/0018/001847/184755E.pdf
15 US National Commission for UNESCO (available at: www.state.gov/p/io/ UNESCO/charter/index.htm).
16 Kerstin Martens, "Non-governmental Organization as Corporatist Mediator? An Analysis of NGOs in the UNESCO System." *Global Society* 15, no. 4 (2001): 387–404.
17 James N. Rosenau, "Governance, Order, and Change in World Politics," in *Governance Without Government: Order and Change in World Politics*, ed. James N. Rosenau and Ernst-Otto Czempiel (Cambridge: Cambridge University Press, 1992).

1 UNESCO's organizational history and structure

1 Quoted in *The UNESCO Courier*, "Attention of World Fixed on UNESCO." (Paris: United Nations Educational, Scientific and Cultural Organization, February 1948), Vol. 1, No. 1, p. 8.
2 IIIC was the institutional home for the League's International Committee for Intellectual Cooperation created in 1922.
3 Quoted in Richard Hoggart, *An Idea and Its Servants: UNESCO from Within* (New York: Oxford University Press, 1978), 26.
4 Lord Ritchie-Calder, "Two Decades in the World of Science," *UNESCO Courier*, July-August 1966: 8.
5 James P. Sewell, *UNESCO and World Politics: Engaging in International Relations* (Princeton, N.J.: Princeton University Press, 1975), 45.
6 Julian Huxley, *UNESCO: Its Purpose and Its Philosophy* (Washington, DC: American Council of Public Affairs, 1947), 25–26.
7 See Steve Hughes and Nigel Haworth, *The International Labour Organization (ILO): Coming in From the Cold* (London: Routledge, 2010).
8 Peter I. Hajnal, *Guide to UNESCO* (London: Oceana Publishers, 1983), 57.
9 Sewell, *UNESCO and World Politics*, 135.
10 For UNDP, see Stephen Browne, *United Nations Development Programme* (London: Routledge, 2011).
11 Sewell, *UNESCO and World Politics*, 141.
12 The phrase is attributed to a US ambassador to the UN in the early 1970s; from a Robert Cox quote in Hajnal, *Guide to UNESCO*, 21.
13 René Maheu, "UNESCO's 20 Years," *UNESCO Courier*, July-August 1966: 4.
14 See Sakiko Fukuda-Parr, *Millennium Development Goals (MDGs): For a People-centered Development Agenda* (London: Routledge, forthcoming).
15 For the WTO, see Bernard Hoekman and Petros C. Mavroidis, *World Trade Organization: Law, Economics, Politics* (London: Routledge, 2007).
16 Cited in Sagarika Dutt, *UNESCO and a Just World Order* (New York: Nova Science Publishers, 2002), 11. The literature review is on pages 8–15.
17 Hoggart, *An Idea and its Servants*, 59.

18 UNESCO, "General introduction to the standard-setting instruments of UNESCO" (available at: http://portal.UNESCO.org/en/ev.php-URL_ID=2 3772&URL_DO=DO_PRINTPAGE&URL_SECTION=201.html).

19 UNESCO (available at http://portal.UNESCO.org/en/ev.php-URL_ID=120 25&URL_DO=DO_TOPIC&URL_SECTION=-471.html).

20 Martha Finnemore, "International Organizations as Teachers of Norms: The United Nations Educational, Scientific and Cultural Organization and Science Policy," *International Organization* 47, no. 4 (Autumn 1993): 565–97.

21 Hoggart, *An Idea and Its Servants*, 20.

22 Given the language regarding "Education for All" in the UNESCO Preamble, the 1990 initiative is regarded as a relaunch of this initiative.

23 Hoggart, *An Idea and Its Servants*, 63.

24 For the US UNESCO charter, see: www.state.gov/p/io/UNESCO/charter/index.htm

25 US General Accounting Office, *Improvements Needed in UNESCO's Management, Personnel, Financial, and Budgeting Practices*, GAO/NSIAD—85–32 (Washington, DC: US General Accounting Office, 1984).

26 Richard Hoggart is a British academic famous for having founded the Centre for Contemporary Cultural Studies at Birmingham University.

27 Hoggart, *An Idea and Its Servants*, 133.

28 Internal Oversight Service Evaluation Section, *Evaluation of UNESCO's Recruitment Policy and Practice* (Paris, UNESCO, IOS/EVS/PI/96 REV. 2, January 2009).

29 Based on interviews at UNESCO headquarters, September–October 2009.

30 Erik Reitzel, *The Symbolic Globe* (Paris, UNESCO Publishing, 2006), 31.

31 Interview with UNESCO official, Paris, 2 October 2009.

32 Interview with UNESCO official, Paris, 2 October 2009.

33 The opposition to Hosny was not just from member states but also from prominent intellectuals, especially in France, who called attention to Hosny's record.

34 *Guardian Weekly*, "UNESCO: Connecting Culture and the People," 6 January 2010 (available at: www.guardianweekly.co.uk/?page=editorial&id=14 12& catID=17).

35 Interview with UNESCO official, 1 October 2009.

36 Ibid.

37 Koïchiro Matsuura, "Information and Dialogue Session with Executive Board, Paris, 25 February 2000," in *A Year of Transition: Selected Speeches—15 November 1999–31 December 2000* (Paris: UNESCO, 2002), 41.

38 For a review of these partnerships, please see *UNESCO-Private Sector Partnership: Making a Difference*, ERC/CFS/MLT/2006/PI/1 (Paris, UNESCO, 2006).

39 UNESCO (available at: http://portal.UNESCO.org/en/ev.php-URL_ID=32 906&URL_DO=DO_TOPIC&URL_SECTION=201.html).

40 Peter Willetts, "From 'Consultative Arrangements' to 'Partnership': The Changing Status of NGOs in Diplomacy at the UN," *Global Governance* 6, no. 2 (2000): 191–214.

41 David Hardman, ed., *Reflections of Our Age: Lectures Delivered at the Opening Session of the UNESCO at the Sorbonne University Paris* (Freeport, N.Y.: Books for Libraries Press, 1949).

42 Jean-Paul Sartre, "The Responsibility of the Writer," in Hardman, 83.

152   *Notes*

43 Kerstin Martens, "Non-governmental Organization as Corporatist Mediator? An Analysis of NGOs in the UNESCO System," *Global Society* 15, no. 4 (2001): 397–98.
44 See "UNESCO Goodwill Ambassadors," at http://portal.UNESCO.org/en/ev. php-URL_ID=4053&URL_DO=DO_TOPIC&URL_SECTION=201.html
45 Hoggart, *An Idea and Its Servants*, 102.

2 Prioritizing education

1 Jacques Delors, "Education the Necessary Utopia," in International Commission for Education in the Twenty-first Century, *Learning: The Treasure Within* (Paris: UNESCO Publishing, 1998), 11.
2 Roger-Pol Droit, *Humanity in the Making: Overview of the Intellectual History of UNESCO 1945–2005* (Paris: UNESCO Publishing, 2005), 63, 74, 80.
3 Richard Jolly, Louis Emmrij, and Thomas G. Weiss, *UN Ideas That Changed the World* (Bloomington: Indiana University Press, 2009).
4 Jolly et al., *UN Ideas*, 86.
5 See, for example, Yvonne Donders and Vladimir Volodon, eds., *Human Rights in Education, Science and Culture: Legal Development and Challenges* (Paris: UNESCO Publishing, 2007).
6 J. K. Galbraith cited in Fons Coomans, "Content and Scope of the Right to Education as a Human Right and Obstacles to Its Realisation" in Donders and Volodon, *Human Rights in Education, Science and Culture*, 185.
7 Archibald Macleish, "Can We Educate for World Peace?," *UNESCO Courier*, October 1985: 27.
8 There are 650 UNRWA schools in Gaza and elsewhere. The United States is the largest bilateral donor, giving $154 million in 2007.
9 Ritchie Calder, "From Dream to Plan of Action." *UNESCO Courier*, December 1956: 12.
10 UNESCO Convention Against Discrimination in Education (available at: http://portal.unesco.org/en/ev.php-URL_ID=12949&URL_DO=DO_TOPIC&URL_SECTION=201.html).
11 Paulo Freire, *The Pedagogy of the Oppressed* (New York: Continuum, 2000). Also see J. P. Singh, "Paulo Freire: Possibilities for Dialogic Communication in a Market-Driven Information Age," Key Thinkers in the Information Age Series, *Information, Communication, and Society* 11, no. 5 (2008): 699–726.
12 Irina Bokova, "Address by Mrs Irina Bokova, Director-General of UNESCO on the Occasion of the Opening of the Sixth UNESCO International Conference on Adult Education (CONFINTEA VI)," Belém, Brazil, 1 December 2009 (available at http://unesdoc.unesco.org/Ulis/cgi-bin/ulis.pl?database=&lin=1& futf8=1& ll=1&gp=&look=default&sc1=1&sc2= 1&nl=1&req=2&ds=adult%20education).
13 "The Mind Awakening," *UNESCO Courier*, August-September 1971: 18–20.
14 United Nations Economic Commission for Africa and UNESCO, *Conference of African States on the Development of Education in Africa: Final Report*, 15–25 May 1961 (available at: www.unesco.org/education/nfsunesco/pdf/ABABA_E.PDF).
15 Vincenzo Pavone, *From the Labyrinth of the World to the Paradise of the Heart: Science and Humanism in UNESCO's Approach to Globalization* (Lanham, Md.: Lexington Books, 2008), 165.

16 "Preamble—World Declaration on Education for All" (available at www. unesco.org/education/efa/ed_for_all/background/jomtien_declaration.shtml).
17 Cynthia Gutman, "A Global Campaign," *UNESCO Courier*, March 2000.
18 Karen Mundy, "Education for All and the New Development Compact," *Review of Education* 52, nos 1–2 (2006): 23–48.
19 Mundy "Education for All and the New Development Compact"; and Karen Mundy "'Education for All' and the Global Governors," in *Who Governs the Globe*, ed. Deborah D. Avant, Martha Finnemore, and Susan K. Sell (Cambridge: Cambridge University Press, 2010).
20 See www.campignforeducation.org
21 Sakkio Fukuda-Parr, "Millennium Development Goals: Why They Matter," *Global Governance* 10, no. 4 (2004): 397.
22 The World Bank group, *Millennium Development Goals*, at http://ddp-ext. worldbank.org/ext/GMIS/gdmis.do?siteId=2& menuId=LNAV01
23 Organization for Economic Co-operation and Development, *Millennium Development Goals*, www.oecd.org/department/0,3355,en_2649_34585_1_1_ 1_1_1,00.html
24 Kevin Watkins, Samer Al-Samarrai, Nicole Bella, Marc Philip Boua Liebnitz, Mariela Buonomo, Stuart Cameron, Alison Clayson, Diederick de Jongh, Anna Haas, Julia Heiss, François Leclercq, Anaïs Loizillon, Leila Loupis, Patrick Montjourides, Karen Moore, Claudine Mukizwa, Paula Razquin, Pauline Rose, Sophie Schlondorff, and Suhad Varin, *EFA Global Monitoring Report 2010: Reaching the Marginalized* (Paris: UNESCO Publishing, 2010).
25 Global Campaign for Education, "EFA in Crisis as Universal Primary Education Falls off Target," available at: www.campaignforeducation.org
26 This paragraph is based on interviews with UNESCO officials, 24 September–5 October 2009, Paris.
27 Mundy, "Education for All and the New Development Compact," 25.
28 Interviews with UNESCO officials, 24 September–5 October 2009, Paris.

3 Making science

1 Martha Finnemore, "International Organizations as Teachers of Norms: The United Nations Educational, Scientific, and Cultural Organization and Science Policy," *International Organization* 47, no. 4 (Autumn 1993): 566.
2 Finnemore, "International Organizations," 585.
3 Jurgen Hillig, "Helping Hands, Guiding Principles: Science and Technology Policies," in P. Petitjean, V. Zharov, G. Glaser, J. Richardson, B. de Paridac, and G. Archibald, eds., *Sixty Years of Science at UNESCO, 1945–2005* (Paris: UNESCO Publishing, 2006), 434–51.
4 Bruno de Padirac, "Hard Talk: The Controversy Surrounding UNESCO's Contribution to the Management of the Scientific Enterprise, 1945–2005," In Petitjean et al., *Sixty Years of Science at UNESCO*, 477.
5 Laurence M. Gould, "Science and the Culture of Our time," *UNESCO Courier* 1963, reprinted in Roger-Pol Droit, *Humanity in the Making: Overview of the Intellectual History of UNESCO, 1945–2005* (Paris: UNESCO Publishing, 2005), 87.
6 *The New UNESCO Sourcebook for Science Teaching*, revised in 1973, can be downloaded from: unesdoc.UNESCO.org/images/0000/000056/005641E.pdf

7 CAME drafting committee document for February 1945, cited in James P. Sewell, *UNESCO and World Politics: Engaging in International Relations* (Princeton, N.J.: Princeton University Press, 1975), 53.

8 For a critique, see Peter Lengyel, *International Social Science: The UNESCO Experience* (New Brunswick, N.J.: Transaction Books, 1986). Peter Lengyel resigned in 1984 from UNESCO after three decades of service. On page 84 he notes that between 1981 and 1994, SHS lost one-third of its staff either due to resignations or transfers within UNESCO.

9 De Padirac, "Hard Talk," 480.

10 "About ICSU," at www.icsu.org/5_abouticsu/INTRO.php

11 Petitijean et al., *Sixty Years of Science at UNESCO*, 559–60.

12 Thanks to Reneé Marlin-Bennett for this definition of synchrotron light.

13 Executive Board, *Report by the Director-General on the Conclusions and Recommendations of the Expert Team on the Overview of Major Programmes II and III.* Paris: UNESCO, 176/EX 7, 5 April 2007.

14 Executive Board, *Report by the Director-General*, 7.

15 Based on interviews with UNESCO officials, Paris, 24 September–5 October 2009.

16 "Culture of Peace: What Is It?" Available at http://www3.UNESCO.org/iycp/uk/uk_sum_cp.htm

17 For an elaboration of the various phases of the Culture of Peace program, see Vincenzo Pavone, *From the Labyrinth of the World to the Paradise of the Heart: Science and Humanism in UNESCO's Approach to Globalization* (Lanham, Md.: Lexington Books, 2008), 137–40, 169–76.

18 Pavone, *From the Labyrinth of the World to the Paradise of the Heart*, 176–82.

19 See, for example, the video *MOST—A "Think Tank" for Nations*, available at http://portal.UNESCO.org/shs/en/ev.php-URL_ID=3511&URL_DO=DO_TOPIC&URL_SECTION=201.html

20 Quoted in Patrick Petitjean, "Giving Science for Peace a Chance: The Post-War International Laboratory Project," in Petitjean et al., *Sixty Years of Science at UNESCO*, 53.

21 Susan Turner, "Rocky Road to Success: A New History of the International Geoscience Program (IGCP)," in Petitjean et al., *Sixty Years of Science at UNESCO*, 297–314.

22 For a summary of the negotiations, see Howard Raiffa, *The Art and Science of Negotiation* (Cambridge, Mass.: Harvard University Press, 1982), chapter 18.

23 Finnemore, "International Organizations as Teachers of Norms."

24 Anne-Marie Slaughter, *A New World Order* (Princeton, N.J.: Princeton University Press, 2004).

25 *Nature*, "What's Wrong with UNESCO," *Nature* 461, no. 7263, 24 September 2009.

26 Based on interviews with UNESCO officials, Paris, 24 September–5 October 2009.

4 The prominence of culture

1 BBC News, "Bulgarian Chosen to Head UNESCO," 22 September 2009; and BBC News, "Egypt Loser Condemns UNESCO Vote," 23 September 2009.

2 Laurent Lévi-Strauss, "Impact of Recent Developments in the Notion of Cultural Heritage on the World Heritage Convention," *World Culture*

Report 2000: Cultural Diversity, Conflict and Pluralism (Paris: UNESCO Publishing, 2000), 155.

3 Quoted in Arjo Klamer and David Throsby, "Paying for the Past: The Economics of Cultural Heritage," *World Culture Report 2000: Cultural Diversity, Conflict and Pluralism* (Paris: UNESCO Publishing, 2000), 138–39.

4 Maria Antonella Pelizzari, "From Stone to Paper: Photographs of Architecture and the Traces of History," in Maria Antonella Pelizzari, ed., *Traces of India: Photographs, Architecture, and the Politics of Representation, 1850–1900* (Canadian Center for Architecture and Yale Center for British Art, 2003), 37.

5 Sandra Braman, "Art–State Relations: Art and Power through the Lens of International Treaties," in J. P. Singh, ed., *International Cultural Policies and Power* (Houndmills, UK: Palgrave Macmillan, 2010), 42. Braman shows that international treaties have guarded the status of art in wartime since the Renaissance.

6 Words written on 8 March 1960 and cited in André Malraux, "Behold, Ancient River ... " in Roger-Pol Droit, ed., *Humanity in the Making: Overview of the Intellectual History of UNESCO, 1945–2005* (Paris: UNESCO Publishing, 2005), 134.

7 Bernd von Droste zu Hülshoff, "A Gift from the Past to the Future: Natural and Cultural World Heritage," in P. Petitjean, V. Zharov, G. Glaser, J. Richardson, B. de Paridac, and G. Archibald, eds., *Sixty Years of Science at UNESCO, 1945–2005* (Paris: UNESCO Publishing, 2006), 391.

8 Sagarika Dutt, *UNESCO and a Just World Order* (New York: Nova Science Publishers, 2002), 136–137.

9 Françoise Benhamou, "Heritage," in Ruth Towse, ed., *A Handbook of Cultural Economics* (Cheltenham, UK: Edward Elgar, 2003).

10 J. P. Singh, *Globalizing Arts: Entertainment Industries and Cultural Identity* (New York: Columbia University Press, 2010). Also, see J. P. Singh, "Culture or Commerce? A Comparative Assessment of International Interactions and Developing Countries at UNESCO, WTO, and Beyond," *International Studies Perspectives* 8, no. 1 (2007): 36–53.

11 Isabelle Brianso, "Valorization of World Cultural Heritage in Time of Globalization: Bridges Between Nations and Cultural Power," in J. P. Singh, op. cit., pp. 166–80.

12 Ibid., 174.

13 World Tourism Organization, *Tourism Highlight 2009 Edition*, available at www.e-unwto.org/content/l80322/?p=3232c34e8c044022b6eee219af58f513&pi=5

14 BBC News, "Mostar Bridge Opens With Splash," 23 July 2004.

15 Lyndel Prott, "Defining the Concept of 'Intangible Heritage': Challenges and Prospects," in *World Culture Report 2000*: 156–57.

16 Text of the Convention for the Safeguarding of Intangible Cultural Heritage (available at: www.UNESCO.org/culture/ich/index.php?pg=00006).

17 Randall Mason and Marta de la Torre, "Heritage Conservation and Values in Globalizing Societies," in *World Culture Report 2000*: 172.

18 This paragraph summarizes the history from Noriko Aikawa, "An Historical Overview of the Preparation of the UNESCO International Convention for the Safeguarding of the Intangible Cultural Heritage," *Museum International* 221–22 (May 2004): 137–49.

19 Based on conversations with UNESCO officials, 2007–9.

20 Noriko Aikawa, "Intangible Cultural Heritage: New Safeguarding Approaches," in *World Culture Report 2000*: 174–75.

21 Javier Peréz de Cuéllar, *Our Creative Diversity: Report of the World Commission on Culture and Development* (Paris: UNESCO Publishing, 1995): 15 (available at: unesdoc.UNESCO.org/images/0010/001055/105586e.pdf).

22 Lourdes Arizpe, "The Intellectual History of Culture and Development Institutions," in Vijayendra Rao and Michael Walton, eds., *Culture and Public Action* (Stanford, Calif.: Stanford University Press, 2004), 162–84.

23 Franz Fanon, *The Wretched of the Earth* (New York: Grove Press, 2004), 172.

24 Edward Said, *Orientalism* (New York: Vintage Books, 1978), 40.

25 Peréz de Cuéllar, *Our Creative Diversity*, 15.

26 Samuel P. Huntington, "The Clash of Civilizations?" *Foreign Affairs*, Summer 1993: 22–49.

27 *World Culture Report 1998: Culture, Creativity and Markets* (Paris: UNESCO Publishing, 1998) and *World Culture Report 2000*.

28 Interview with UNESCO official, 5 October 2009.

29 Lourdes Arizpe, "The Intellectual History of Culture and Development Institutions," 175.

30 The negotiation history of cultural industry and related intellectual property issues can be found in J. P. Singh, *Negotiation and the Global Information Economy* (Cambridge: Cambridge University Press, 2008).

31 MFN or most favored nation clauses in international trade mean that no nation is to be discriminated against in application of trade measures. An MFN exemption thus allows Europeans to discriminate against any nation, in this case the United States.

32 The European Union negotiates as a single entity in trade negotiations at the WTO. However, its single position often reveals fissures. The United Kingdom, the biggest cultural products exporter in the EU, and countries such as Denmark and the Netherlands, are reluctant to go along with protectionist measures. At UNESCO, EU member states vote individually as culture is not considered a European Commission but a national competency.

33 Available at unesdoc.UNESCO.org/images/0012/001271/127160m.pdf

34 Delegation Permanente de France, 16 October 2002, Annex 1.

35 Jane Kelsey, *Serving Whose Interests?: The Political Economy of Trade in Services Agreements* (London: Routledge-Cavendish, 2008), 232.

36 World Trade Organization, 30 June 2005. Communication from Hong Kong, China, Japan, Mexico, The Separate Customs Territory of Taiwan, Penghu, Kinmen and Matsu; and United States. Joint Statement on the Negotiation of Audiovisual Services. TNS/S/W/49. Available at http://portal.UNESCO. org/en/ev.php-URL_ID=31038&URL_DO=DO_TOPIC&URL_SECTION =201.html.

37 WTO, 30 June 2005.

38 *UNESCO World Report: Investing in Cultural Diversity and Intercultural Dialogue* (Paris: UNESCO Publishing, 2009). Available at: unesdoc. UNESCO.org/images/0018/001847/184755E.pdf

5 Debating global communication orders

1 Hedley Bull, *The Anarchical Society: A Study of Order in World Politics* (New York: Columbia University Press, 1995).

2 Clare Wells, *The UN, UNESCO and the Politics of Knowledge* (New York: St. Martin's Press, 1987), chapter 4. The analysis of the US efforts presented below borrows a great deal from Wells' description.
3 Clare Wells, *The UN, UNESCO and the Politics of Knowledge*, 61.
4 William Preston Jr., Edward S. Herman, and Herbert I Schiller, *Hope and Folly: The United States and UNESCO 1945–1985* (Minneapolis: University of Minnesota Press, 1989), 59.
5 Preston et al., *Hope and Folly*, 59.
6 John A. Lent, *The New World and International Information Order: A Resource Guide and Bibliography* (Singapore: Asian Mass Communication and Research and Information Center, 1982), 3.
7 Thomas L. McPhail, *Electronic Colonialism: The Future of International Broadcasting and Communication* (Beverly Hills, Calif.: Sage Publications, 1981), 93.
8 For UNCTAD, see Ian Taylor and Karen Smith, *United Nations Conference on Trade and Development* (London: Routledge, 2007).
9 Kaarle Nordenstreng, *The Mass Media Declaration of UNESCO* (Norwood, N.J.: Ablex Publishing, 1983).
10 Steve Biko, "Black Consciousness and the Quest for a True Humanity." Available at http://www.assatashakur.org/forum/carriers-torch/1399-black-consciousness-quest-true-humanity-steve-biko.html
11 Edward Said, *Orientalism* (New York: Vintage Books, 1978), 40.
12 For provocative discussions of the debates surrounding NIEO, see Jagdish Bhagwati, ed., *The New International Economic Order: The North South Debate* (Cambridge, Mass.: MIT Press, 1977); and the Brandt Commission, *A Program for Survival* (New York: United Nations, 1980). For a critique of NIEO, see Stephen Krasner, *Structural Conflict: The Third World Against Global Liberalism* (Berkeley: University of California Press, 1985).
13 David Lerner, *The Passing of Traditional Society: Modernizing the Middle East* (Glencoe, Ill.: Free Press, 1958), viii.
14 An innovative, yet controversial and somewhat reactionary figure, Schramm aided in the development and growth of many early schools of communication study, specifically at Iowa (1943–47), Illinois (1947–55), Stanford (1955–73), and at the East-West Communication Institute, University of Hawaii.
15 Rita Cruise O'Brien, ed., *Information, Economics and Power: The North-South Dimension* (Boulder, Colo.: Westview Press, 1983); and Hamid Mowlana, *International Flow of Information: A Global Report and Analysis* (Paris: UNESCO, 1985).
16 Oliver Boyd-Barrett, "Global Communication Orders," in Bella Mody, ed., *International and Development Communication: A 21st Century Perspective* (Thousand Oaks, Calif.: Sage Publications, 2003), 39.
17 The MacBride Commission, *Many Voices, One World: Towards a New, More Just, and More Efficient World Information and Communication Order* (Lanham, Md.: Rowman & Littlefield, 1980), 254–55.
18 On a more general level in communications, this is reflected in the writings of Johann Galtung and Paul Streeten. See Johann Galtung, "The New International Order: Economics and Communications," and Paul Streeten, "The Conflict Between the Communication Gaps and Suitability Gaps," in Meheroo Jussawalla and Don M. Lamberton, eds., *Communication Economics and Development* (Hawaii: East-West Center, 1982).

19 Hamid Mowlana and Laurie J. Wilson, *The Passing of Modernity: Communication and the Transformation of Society* (New York: Longman, 1990), 60.
20 Sean McBride and Colleen Roach, "The New International Order," in G. Gerbner, H. Mowlana, and K. Nordenstreng, eds., *The Global Media Debate: Its Rise, Fall and Renewal* (Norwood, N.J.: Ablex), 7.
21 McPhail, *Electronic Colonialism*, 16.
22 McPhail, *Electronic Colonialism*, 90.
23 The MacBride Commission, *Many Voices, One World*, 3.
24 The MacBride Commission, *Many Voices, One World*, 275.
25 Interview in Paris, 5 October 2009.
26 The Tunis Agenda for the Information Society can be accessed at: www.itu.int/wsis/docs2/tunis/off/6rev1.html
27 Communication and Information Sector, *Communication and Information Programmes* (Paris: UNESCO, 2005).
28 UNESCO World Report, *Towards Knowledge Societies* (Paris: UNESCO Publishing, 2005).
29 Please see J. P. Singh, *Negotiation and the Global Information Economy* (Cambridge: Cambridge University Press, 2008). Chapter 6.
30 Please see a provocative paper I wrote on rethinking Paulo Freire's ideas in a market-driven context: J. P. Singh, "Paulo Freire: Possibilities for Dialogic Communication in a Market-Driven Information Age," Key Thinkers in the Information Age series, *Information, Communication, and Society* 11, no. 5 (2008): 699–726.
31 Interview with a UNESCO official in Paris, 2 October 2009.
32 The MacBride Commission, *Many Voices, One World*, 281. These comments are part of Appendix I of the report that gathers "General Comments" on the report from members of the Commission.

6 Reflections and possibilities

1 Ramón-Luis Acuña, "A Culture of Peace," *Le Monde Diplomatique* (English edition), November 1999 (available at: http://mondediplo.com/1999/11/).
2 Interview with UNESCO official in Paris, 2 October 2009.
3 Richard Jolly, Louis Emmerij, and Thomas G. Weiss, *UN Ideas That Changed the World* (Bloomington: Indiana University Press, 2009), 221.
4 Frank Richard Cowell, "Planning the Organization of UNESCO, 1942–46: A Personal Record," reprinted from *Journal of World History* 10, no. 1 (1966), in Pierre Sané, ed., *What UNESCO for the Future* (Paris: UNESCO Publishing, 2006), xix.
5 Cowell, "Planning the Organization of UNECO," xx.
6 Cowell, "Planning the Organization of UNECO," iv.
7 Sir Sarvapali (sic) Radhakrishnan, "Indian Culture," in David Hardman, ed., *Reflections of Our Age: Lectures Delivered at the Opening Session of UNESCO at the Sorbonne University Paris* (Freeport, N.Y.: Books for Libraries Press, 1949).
8 James P. Sewell, *UNESCO and World Politics: Engaging in International Relations* (Princeton, N.J.: Princeton University Press, 1975), 5.
9 *Guardian Weekly*, "UNESCO: Connecting Culture and the People," 6 January 2010.

10 Peter Lengyel, *International Social Science: The UNESCO Experience* (New Brunswick, N.J.: Transaction Books, 1986), 93.
11 *Guardian Weekly*, "UNESCO: Connecting Culture and the People."
12 Tu Weiming, no title, in Pierre Sané, ed., *What UNESCO for the Future*, 181.
13 Thomas G. Weiss, Tatiana Carayannis, and Richard Jolly, "The 'Third' United Nations," *Global Governance* 15 (2009): 123–42.
14 Inis L. Claude, *Swords into Plowshares: Problems and Prospects of International Organization* (New York: Random House, 1956).
15 "The UNESCO Blunder," *New York Sun*, 13 September 2002; Brett D. Schaefer, "Not the Time for the United States to Rejoin UNESCO," *The Heritage Foundation*, 17 January 2001; and George F. Will, "Dimwitted Nod to 'Diversity,'" *Washington Post*, 12 October 2005.
16 Gabrielle Capla, "UNESCO: Privatised and Dismantled," *Le Monde Diplomatique*, September 2009 (available at http://mondediplo.com/2009/09/08unesco). She cites from an underground report circulated in UNESCO: "Matsuura and His Clique: From Cover-up to Take-over," *UNESCO in Danger Report*, no. 1, part 1, September 2008.
17 See, for example, the various six-year planning C/4 documents and contrast them with the budgetary priorities of the C/5 documents that assign the biennial budgets to specific programs.
18 Based on interviews, 24 September–5 October 2009.
19 Richard Hoggart, *An Idea and Its Servants: UNESCO From Within* (New York: Oxford University Press, 1978), chapter 6.
20 David Held, Anthony McGrew, David Goldblatt, and Jonathan Perraton, *Global Transformations: Politics, Economics and Culture* (Stanford, Calif.: Stanford University Press, 1999).
21 Daniel Bell, "Introduction," in Simon Nora and Alain Minc, eds., *The Computerization of Society* (Cambridge, Mass.: MIT Press, 1980).
22 James N. Rosenau, *Turbulence in World Politics: A Theory of Change and Continuity* (Princeton, N.J.: Princeton University Press, 1990). For applications to technological transformations, see James N. Rosenau and J. P. Singh, eds., *Information Technologies and Global Politics: The Changing Scope of Power and Governance* (Albany, N.Y.: State University of New York Press, 2002).
23 Hoggart, *An Idea and Its Servants*, 161.
24 Hoggart, *An Idea and Its Servants*, 193–94.
25 Interview with UNESCO official, 2 October 2009.

Select bibliography

Lourdes Arizpe, *World Culture Report: Cultural Diversity, Conflict and Pluralism* (Paris: UNESCO Publishing, 2000). A masterpiece that builds on the interdisciplinary understanding of *Our Creative Diversity* report. It brings together essays from interdisciplinary perspectives both within and outside of UNESCO.

Sagarika Dutt, *UNESCO and a Just World Order* (New York: Nova Scotia Publishers, 2002). This book provides an excellent summary in its first three chapters of UNESCO's evolution and then presents an intellectual history of UNESCO's various sectors and current initiatives drawing upon various published sources.

Peter Hajnal, *Guide to UNESCO* (London: Oceana Publications, Inc., 1983). Although somewhat dated, this book provides an excellent summary of UNESCO's secretariat, organization, and major initiatives and conventions.

Richard Hoggart, *An Idea and Its Servants: UNESCO From Within* (New York: Oxford University Press, 1978). This lively account, a memoir of sorts for Hoggart, who served as Assistant Director-General at UNESCO, is a must read for anyone wishing to understand the inner workings and intrigues within UNESCO. Written before the United States and United Kingdom left the organization, this book written by an academic who shaped critical and cultural studies globally, provides a perspective on UNESCO's politicization and inefficiency in the 1970s.

Julian Huxley, *UNESCO: Its Purpose and Its Philosophy* (Washington, DC: American Council of Public Affairs, 1947). This short book remains a classic. It was meant to become an official statement of UNESCO's early mission but was criticized by the Eastern bloc for being propagandistic and by conservatives in the West for being atheistic.

Internal Oversight Service Evaluation Section, *Evaluation of UNESCO's Recruitment Policy and Practice* (Paris, UNESCO, IOS/EVS/PI/96 REV. 2, January 2009). A sobering reflection on how far UNESCO has come or how far it has to go with its recruiting practices.

The MacBride Commission, *Many Voices, One World: Towards a New, More Just, and More Efficient World Information and Communication Order* (Lanham, Md.: Rowman & Littlefield, 2004/1980). This is the classic work of UNESCO's International Commission for the Study of Communication Problems. Coming in the midst of the New World Information Communication Order debates, this study is an important and balanced treatise on the role of communication and its infrastructures among societies and nations.

Vincenzo Pavone, *From the Labyrinth of the World to the Paradise of the Heart: Science and Humanism in UNESCO's Approach to Globalization* (Lanham, Md.: Lexington Books, 2008). This is the book to read to see how humanist philosophical ideas have guided UNESCO's mission. It offers a great degree of detail on Director-General Federico Mayor's term.

Javier Peréz de Cuéllar, *Our Creative Diversity: Report of the World Commission on Culture and Development* (Paris: UNESCO Publishing, 1995). This report was meant to bring in cultural factors into a study of development and built on similar initiatives elsewhere, especially in the UNDP. Its findings led to the two *World Culture Reports* from UNESCO in 1998 and 2000 and it was cited frequently in the debates on cultural diversity in the first decade of this century at UNESCO.

Patrick Petitjean, V. Zharov, G. Glaser, J. Richardson, B. de Paridac, and G. Archibald, eds., *Sixty Years of Science at UNESCO, 1945–2005* (Paris: UNESCO Publishing, 2006). An excellent account of UNESCO's natural science sectors in its first 60 years, written mostly by former and current UNESCO officials. The book is comprehensive and helps one appreciate the enormity of UNESCO's enterprise in natural sciences.

Roger Pol-Droit, *Humanity in the Making: Overview of the Intellectual History of UNESCO 1945–2005* (Paris: UNESCO Publishing, 2005). This is a short illustrated intellectual history of UNESCO, issued at the organization's 60th anniversary, and offers excerpts from various documents and speeches that have shaped UNESCO's history along with an expert commentary from French philosopher Roger Pol-Droit.

William Preston, Jr., Edward S. Herman, and Herbert I. Schiller, *Hope and Folly: The United States and UNESCO 1945–1985* (Minneapolis: University of Minnesota Press, 1989). A highly readable account from the NWICO debate's academic protagonists in the United States, who explain how and why, from their perspective, the United States misunderstood and politicized itself over NWICO and earlier communication issues in UNESCO.

Pierre Sané, ed., *What UNESCO for the Future* (Paris: UNESCO Publishing, 2006). This book includes short essays from global leaders bearing upon the question in the title at UNESCO's 60th anniversary celebrations.

James P. Sewell, *UNESCO and World Politics: Engaging in International Relations* (Princeton, N.J.: Princeton University Press, 1975). This book details carefully the politics, negotiations, and organizational challenges for UNESCO. The attention to detail is especially masterful in delineating UNESCO's evolving agenda.

The UNESCO Courier. This monthly magazine, published from UNESCO and now available online, provides an important resource for researching the organization's affairs since its inception. Available at: http://portal.unesco.org/en/ev. php-URL_ID=44481&URL_DO=DO_TOPIC&URL_SECTION=201.html

Index

Dakar Conference (2000) 22, 47, 59–66
declarations (from UNESCO) 20–22; in
communication 115–18; in culture
102–3; in education 52, 58, 60; in
sciences 68–69, 73, 77
Delors Commission, *see Learning, The
Treasure Within*
digital divide 26, 76, 109, 121
Director-General 31–32, 36–39
discrimination and oppression issues
49–52, 54–55, 99, 114
Dutt, Sagraika 19, 92

Economic and Social Council
(ECOSOC) 6–9, 16, 43, 75
Education for All (EFA) 10, 22, 24, 47,
54, 57–66
Einstein, Albert 2, 13
Enlightenment 1,4, 7, 19, 68; *see also*
humanism
environmental issues 4, 25, 36, 69–70,
74–79, 85, 90, 94; *see also*
sustainability issues
ethics issues 2, 9, 11, 25–26, 126; in
culture 99, 103; in journalism 118,
121, *see also* bioethics; in science
71–74, 79
eugenics 4, 14, 73–74
Europe 56, 75, 101–2. 119
European Commission 40, 101
European Union 79, 103, 120
Evans, Luther 16, 38
Executive Board 13, 20. 29–32, 38, 40,
44, 67, 82, 95, 133

Fanon, Franz 56, 99, 114
Fauré, Edgard 57, 60, *see also
Learning to Be*
field offices (UNESCO) 28, 33, 36, 40,
65–66, 70, 134
film issues 98, 100–101, 104, 107, 130
Florence Agreement 111
Food and Agricultural Organization
(FAO) 42, 75, 78–79, 123
France 5, 12, 17, 19, 45, 119, 134;
cultural issues 75, 101–6
Fulbright, Senator 4, 128

Gates Foundation 41
gender issues 8, 26, 41, 59, 62, 64, 121,
133
General Agreement on Tariffs and
Trade, *see* WTO

General Agreement on Trade in
Services (GATS) 101, *see also* WTO
General Conference; and communication
111, 116–19; and culture 91, 95, 98,
104, 106; and education 58; and
sciences 67, 71–78, 81; organization
and functions 12, 20–22, 31–32,
36–45, 128–29
General History of Africa 27, 56
genetics and genome issues 25, 69, 73–74
geosciences 74, 79
Global Campaign for Education
61–63, 65
global compact 41, 62, 127
goodwill ambassadors 9, 45, 63
Group of 77 (G-77) 98

Heritage Foundation 119–20
heritage, *see* world heritage
Hesse, Herman 19
Hobbes, Thomas 19, 70, 129
Hoggart, Richard 19, 22, 29, 33, 45,
133, 135
Hong Kong 106
Hosny, Farouk 29, 39
human rights 6, 16, 18–22, 25, 27, 29,
132; in communication 110, 118–19; in
culture 85, 102, 104; in sciences 69–73,
77, 81; International Covenant on
Economic, Social and Cultural Rigths
(ICESR) 50; Universal Declaration of
Human Rights (UDHR) 48–49, 58
humanism 1–5, 14, 19, 68, 77, 111,
126–32
Hungary 16
Huxley, Julian 1–6, 14, 24, 38, 72, 112,
128–29

idealism, *see* humanism
India 12, 96, 111, 128
Indonesia 87, 97
Inernational Network for Cultural
Diversity (INCD) 104
intellectuals, role in UNESCO 2, 7–9,
26–29, 43–44, 125–27
International Corporation for
Assigned Names and Numbers 124
International Council of Monuments
(ICOMOS) 87–88
International Council of Museums
(ICOM) 9, 27, 44
International Council of Science
(ICSU) 9, 13, 70, 74, 78